SOWING TI LEAVES

second edition

SOWING TI LEAVES

WRITINGS BY MULTICULTURAL WOMEN

edited by

MITSUYE YAMADA

SARIE SACHIE HYLKEMA

MCWW Press Irvine

Design consultant, Hedi Yamada

Diana Azar: "Have-A-Heart Traps" from The Elephant-ear
(Irvine, CA: Irvine Valley College, 1988).
Sarie Sachie Hylkema: "Japanese Girl" from The Webs We Weave
(Laguna Beach, CA: Literary Arts Press, 1986).
Mitsuye Yamada: "For Priscilla" and "My Home Town This Earth"
from Desert Run; Poems and Stories
(Latham, NY: Kitchen Table: Women of Color Press, 1988)

First Edition, 1990
Second Edition. 1991

ISBN 0-9630978-0-6
Library of Congress Catalogue Number: 89-92359

Published by
MCWW Press
6151 Sierra Bravo Road, Irvine, California 92715

Acknowledgments

Grateful acknowledgment is made to our translators:
Richard Liao, Lecturer in Chinese Languages
in the Department of East Asian Languages and Literature
at University of California, Irvine;
Julian Palley, poet and Professor of Spanish Literature
at the University of California, Irvine, CA,
and Yoko Shima, poet and Professor of Literature
at Daitobunka University, Tokyo, Japan.

Thanks to André Mouchard for his help with the typing and his
invaluable expertise on the word processor.

Thanks to the following donors for their contributions:
Joe and Judy Yasutake, Tosh and Fumi Yasutake, Ken Stueck,
and Mitzi Bond. Special thanks to Fusae Munemitsu for her
contribution to this publication in memory of her late husband,
Charles Munemitsu.

This printing of *Sowing Ti Leaves,*
Writings by MultiCultural Women is supported by a grant from
the California Arts Council Multi-Cultural
Entry Grant and by a generous matching grant by Robert
Yamafuji of Corbin Yamafuji Partners, Inc., Irvine, CA.

CONTENTS

MORE POEMS

SHORT STORIES

ESSAYS

BIOGRAPHICAL NOTES

INTRODUCTION

by Mitsuye Yamada

Sowing Ti Leaves. The metaphor recalls an array of images to reflect the textures of our separate lives. We are women whose lives have been formed out of a variety of cultures. Some of these images are in community, bringing us together; others in opposition, serving as stimuli or catalysts. Our dominant image is *sowing.* We hear *sowing*: planting, dispersing, broadcasting and even squandering with abandon. We picture *sewing*: piecing together patches of fabric from our lives as women have done for centuries or patching things up, another activity that has been part of our traditional role. We taste *ti leaves*: edible leaves which women in the Pacific Islands still use to make neat packages of wrapped rice, vegetables and meats for family and friends, putting things in neat order, gathering and nurturing those around us. Or we savor the more familiar *tea*: a mild beverage women were expected to serve during leisurely afternoons along with casual conversation and amiable company. On the other hand *tea ceremony*: ritual pouring and drinking, a solitary inward journey into oneself in the company of others. Or fragrant *tea leaves*: our fortunes floating at random in our individual cups. There may be others. In this collection we are seeing these cups together for the first time. This collection may tell us as well as our readers how to interpret our collective future.

Sowing Ti Leaves; Writings by MultiCultural Women represents the writings of the MultiCultural Women Writers (MCWW) who met at least once or twice a month in each others' homes for the past nine years. Our membership fluctuated through the years as did our goals. We are an eclectic group, ranging in age from twenty-something to sixty-something. Our ancestral ties are African, Argentinian, Chinese, East Indian, Hawaiian, Italian, Japanese, Jewish, Lebanese, and Okinawan. We had originally called ourselves the Asian Pacific American

Women Writers of Orange County, but in a few years we saw the need to expand our vision to include other ethnic women who also carry the weight of stereotypes imposed on them by the dominant society.

We met at first with vague hopes of "writing about the condition of our lives, for mutual support, thoughtful critiquing and personal growth." We met early in the evening after work, for we are, for the most part, full-time working women. We shared food, drinks, thoughts about our splintered pasts and hopes for a more harmonious future. During these meetings, we talked, wrote, sometimes confronted each other, at times testily (or didn't when we should have), frequently laughed and cried together, and occasionally performed together at poetry readings.

For purposes of communicating with each other, English has been our common language during our meetings, though English is not the primary language for a few of us. Some of our works in this collection are presented bilingually for we wish to demonstrate that, whatever the language, we share a common experience — our struggles to survive in a majority culture as women. The most valuable lesson we have learned is that our experiences are valid and that they are worth sharing with others. This alone has been empowering for individual members. For us, the writing process was a means of discovering and understanding our own as well as each other's identities. Through eating, talking and writing with our sisters, we found that we share a common female culture.

MCWW members know only too well that we need more than good intentions to realize our goals. Most of us are products of the "mainstream" educational system in the United States and have been seduced in one way or other to be assimilated in order to appear "normal." For the most part, the American educational system did not provide us with a sense of our own ethnic identity, nor did it demonstrate to us how we might be part and parcel of a rich pluralistic American culture. For this reason, "minority" groups have too often put up barriers among themselves, making inter-cultural communication extremely difficult. In MCWW we have tried to create a forum through which we can talk and write about our inner struggles and to bridge those gaps which still exist even among us in this small group. We have persisted through difficult times and have somehow stayed together for almost a decade. This anthology is our first major group undertaking and is only the beginning of other future collective projects.

Sowing Ti Leaves includes personal narratives, poems, essays, and a scholarly study. We found early on during our meetings that personal narratives, such as Susana Saladini's searching narrative in "The Smell of Magic" and Kanwal Yodh's unembellished account in "A Brown Woman's Struggles," were the most direct and natural way to begin our explorations. Some recollections shared for the first time were honed and crafted into poems, such as Janet Jue's story of her Aunt Di Yee in "Poon." Personal anecdotes recalled and retold often turned into critical perceptions as in Sarie Sachie Hylkema's "Victim of Nice" or my essay, "The Cult of the 'Perfect' Language." For women, even scholarly studies are derived directly out of our personal connections. Helen Jaskoski observes in her study of Owl Woman that because society often isolates women socially, books are more important to women than to men in overcoming the boundaries of language and culture.

We hope that our process as well as the product, the collection itself, will be useful for persons presently learning to express themselves in English. We hope that our writings will demonstrate to those struggling within a structured multi-cultural setting (e.g. English-as-a-Second-Language, or remedial English classes) that open exchange of personal experiences is not only energizing, but productive. Also, students in Women's Studies and other disciplines should find these pieces helpful in their understanding of cultures other than their own.

We have included a poem by the late Priscilla Oaks who was a vital force in MCWW before she was taken from us by a drunk driver late one night in an automobile accident. Her "Last Will and Testament" was originally submitted for publication in *The Webs We Weave, an Orange County Anthology* published in 1986, but because the anthology appeared so soon after her death, we chose not to include it in that collection. I can still remember that evening she read "Last Will" to us at one of our meetings; her performance was vintage Priscilla. I can hear her whooping laughter as she read what she considered to be a delicious joke on herself and her family. It is published here for the first time in memory of the once vibrantly alive Priscilla.

Notes to The Second Edition

We have made changes to the first edition. Susana Saladini's "A Smell of Magic" was her first published work in English, but she has since translated her narrative into Spanish, her native language. We now proudly present both versions in this edition. We have also added Alane Hayes' short essay, "I am Black, Does That Make A Difference?" Alane was a new member a year ago when the first edition of the anthology was in production. She has since become an active member of the MultiCultural Women Writers.

A tragedy has struck our group as this second edition goes to press. After her valiant two-year battle, Diana Azar succumbed to cancer. Her contribution to our group has been inspiring. We will miss her.

Diana, unchaste goddess
of chastity
avenger queen,
draws blood from her
sceptre
The looping serpent
goddess
who ties us to
the world out there
un acto de sorpresa
an act of surprise
luz difusa de
the defused light of
eternidad
eternity

To love woman
I need to start with
me
us
you
I celebrate
our past
now
here
every
where

Collective poem by MCWW

1988 Retreat
with Deena Metzger
Topanga, CA

EL AROMA DE LA MAGIA

by *Susana Saladini*

Llegué a este país a la edad de veinticinco años con mi hija de tres. Mujer blanca considerada sola, por no tener la compañia de un hombre. Latina-Americana de ancestros italianos. Mi primera lengua es Castellano. Yo vine a esta tierra de oportunidades a trabajar creyendo que aqui todo era posible. Descubrí que las posibilidades eran mejores para algunas que para otras. Todo era confuso para mí. Algunos me catalogaron como "mujer de color", por ser latina y hablar castellano. Yo, la mujer blanca de clase media descendiente de italianas, maestra recibida en Argentina, Hispana-Parlante, madre responsable, soñadora, curiosa, cristiana, católica, agnóstica me transformé en mujer de color, sirvienta, ama-de-llaves, niñera.

Fue maravilloso haber llegado aquí, al paraíso de las estrellas de cine, las escritoras, los ricos, los políticos influyentes. Siempre quise conocer a los dueños de mi país.

Comencé a trabajar para las "mujeres sin nombre." Al poco tiempo de llegar comprendí que los únicos trabajos disponibles para mí o para otras mujeres en mi situación eran trabajos de campo, fábricas o trabajos domésticos. Elegí estos últimos para poder cuidar a mi hija. Las mujeres sin nombre eran muy generosas para con nosotras. A cambio de trabajar horas extras y/o cuidar a sus hijas mientras limpiaba la casa , sin recibir pago adicional, me permitían traer a mi hija dentro de la casa. Con agrado siempre pagué el precio de esa generosidad,después de todo esto ha sido parte de mi educación. En mi país estamos acostumbradas a pagar por la generosidad de Los Estados Unidos. A veces pagamos con dinero otras con vidas humanas, pero siempre pagamos.

Yo trabajaba largas horas sin hablar con ninguna persona adulta. Quebré ese aislamiento aprendiedo a hablar inglés, aunque llevó años de práctica. Al mismo tiempo aprendí todo lo que pude sobre las otras "gentes de color." Los Afro-

THE SMELL OF MAGIC

by Susana Saladini

I came to this country at the age of twenty-five with my child who was three years old. I was a white woman without a man. My country is in Latin America. My ancestors are Italian. My first language is Spanish. I was called a "woman of color." My confusion was enormous. I came to this land of opportunity where everything was possible — for some better than for others. I was a white middle-class Italian-descent teacher from Argentina, Spanish-speaking, woman-of-color, maid, housekeeper, babysitter, responsible mother, dreamer, curious, Christian, Catholic, agnostic. It was wonderful to be here in Southern California, the land of the movie stars, the wealthy, the writers. I wanted to know the owners of my country.

But I was confused.

I started to work for the women without names. Soon after arriving, I learned that the only available jobs for me (as for many other women in my situation) were field labor, factory work, or housework. I chose the last so that my daughter could be with me. The women without names were very generous to me and my daughter, especially if I worked extra hours without extra pay, or babysat their children free of charge to be able to have my child with me. I gladly paid the price of their generosity. After all, that was part of my upbringing. In my country we always paid for the generosity of the United States, sometimes in money, sometimes in human lives.

I needed to break my isolation. I was working long hours by myself with no adult to talk to. I learned the language after years of practice. Simultaneously, I learned about the "other" people of color—the African Americans whom I knew as Blacks and the Mexican Americans who called themselves Chicanos. I had to learn about the "Blacks" in books, magazines and newspapers because there were not many in Orange County, much less in Newport Beach, Corona del Mar, or Laguna Beach

Americanos, a los que yo conocía como negros y los Mejico-Americanos, algunos de los cuales se llaman a sí mismos Chicanos. La mayoria de lo que aprendí sobre los negros en esos primeros años en çalifornia lo aprendí de periódicos, revistas y televisión pues no eran muchos los afroamericanos que vivían en el condado de Orange especialmente en las ciudades de Newport Beach, Corona del Mar y Laguna Beach donde yo trabajaba para las mujeres sin nombre. Tampoco conocía entonces la realidad de mis hermanas/nos latinoamericanas. Méjico, El Salvador, Guatemala etc. eran para mí países en libros de geografia. Esos libros poco me eseñaron de la entereza moral, la integridad, la valentía, la capacidad de trabajo de las gentes de esos países. Allí encontré la oportunidad de aprender compartiendo experiencias trabajando juntos.

Después de haber trabajado en el aislamiento de las casas de las "mujeres sin nombre por varios años," trabajé para una agencia de empleos domésticos y más tarde tuve mi propia agencia. Buscaba empleos para mujeres como yo y las empleadoras eran mujeres como mis antiguas patronas. Traducia entrenaba y transportaba, haciedo algunos de los trabajos domésticos yo misma.

Las idas y venidas en el automóbil eran nuestros ratos para charlar, reir y contar historias personales. Yo me sentia una mujer de color aunque a ellas les resultaba un tanto extranjera . Algunas de las mujeres sin nombre trataron de hacerme sentir que yo era differente a las trabajadoras casi una de "ellas," (pobre y de clase trabajadora, debo agregar).

Durante este período una gran revelación cambió mi vida: descubrí el Feminismo. Me incorporé al movimiento feminista y finalmente conocí mujeres blancas con nombres propios. Mrs. Roger Brown era en realidad Alice Brown y Roger era su esposo. Identidades y sentimientos nuevos. Me sumergí en un mar turbulento de ideas y contradicciones que aceleraron mi crecimiento intelectual y emocional.

Cuando Mrs. Margiano llamó a mi oficina atendí el llamado en el teléfono de mi escritorio. Nunca supe su primer nombre pero sabía que tenía uno. Solicitó una mucama para la

where I was working for the women with no names. I didn't
know about the Hispanics either. Mexico, El Salvador and
Guatemala were countries in the geography books. Those books
didn't say very much about the real courage, integrity and
endurance of the people from those countries. But here, I was
surrounded by them, learning, sharing experiences, working
together.

After working in the isolation of the homes of the women
without names for several years, I worked for a domestic
employment agency, and later I opened my own agency that
found jobs for women like my former self. I served women who
needed jobs cleaning houses for women like my former
employers. The rides in the car with the women I hired were
times to talk, laugh, and tell personal stories. My workers and I
learned about one another this way. I was feeling like a woman
of color, even though some of them didn't see me that way. I was
foreign to them. Some of the women without names tried to
convince me that I was more like them (only poor and working-
class). I was growing strong in an intricate sea of identities,
feelings, and ideas that contradicted one another.

It was at this time that I had the greatest life-changing
experience: I discovered Feminism. I joined the women's
movement and finally met white women with names. Mrs.
Roger Brown was indeed Alice Brown, and Roger was her
husband.

I was at my desk in my office when Mrs. Margiano called.
I never knew her first name, but I knew she had one. She
requested a weekly maid. I thought that would be ideal for
Noemi to start with. She came from El Salvador not long before
and had asked me for a job. Noemi needed to save money to
bring her children from El Salvador. In her country a war was
going on but not too many people talked about it. In those days
it was called "Insurgency and Subversion." The vocabulary had
changed since then. Now it is called a war. The cruelty and
destruction was always the same. Noemi never talked about her
husband. I didn't ask, and she didn't mention him. She was
living with some relatives in a two bedroom apartment. Two of

limpieza semanal. Pensé en Noemi este sería un buen trabajo para comenzar. Hacía poco tiempo que había llegado de El Salvador y me pidió trabajo. Noemi necesitaba ahorrar dinero para traer a sus hijos que habian quedado en El Salvador. En su país la guerra continuaba aunque muy pocos hablaban de ella en esos términos. Entonces la llamaban "Insurgencia y Subversión." El lenguage ha cambiado, ahora la llaman Guerra pero la crueldad y la destrucción siempre fue la misma. Noemi nunca hablaba de su marido y yo nunca pregunté. Ella vivía con algunos parientes en un departamento de dos habitaciones. Eran muchos y dos de los hombres dormían en el garage. Nunca supe si todos eran en realidad parientes pero era obvio que compartían la pobreza, el orgullo, el deseo de trabajar y la nostalgia por sus familias y las hijas/os que quedaron lejos. Maria, la mucama permanente que vivía en casa de Mrs. Margiano era salvadoreña. Al llegar, en la mañana, Mrs. Margiano me dijo que Maria se encargaria de instruir a Noemi y de traducir lo que fuera necesario. Me fui confiando que todo iría bien.

Volví por Noemi a las 4:30 de la tarde. Mrs Margiano abrió la puerta en persona. Pregunté cómo fue todo, me contestó, OK. pero en forma evasiva y nerviosa. Rapidamente desapareció hacia el interior de la casa . Yo me quedé esperando en el jardín del frente. Cuando Noemi salió de la casa Mrs.Margiano apareció detrás de ella y le gritó ALTO!. Noemi sobresaltada se detuvo a mitad de camino entre la patrona y yo. Con la satisfacción de un detective que está a punto de resolver un caso Mrs. Margiano me ordenó que le revisara la cartera de Noemi. Porqué? Qué pasó? pregunté. Yo no estaba dispuesta a hacer lo que me pedía. "Ella me robó perfume que cuesta $100 la onza", me contestó. Noemi me entregó una pequeña botella de plástico descartada en la que había puesto un poquito de perfume de tres botellitas diferentes. La fragancia estaba arruinada. Mrs Margiano rehusó mi oferta de pagar por el perfume, en cambio me pidió que despidiera a Noemi y que nunca le diera trabajo en ninguna casa del area. Me estaba pidiendo que la castigara negándole el derecho a trabajar. En el auto Noemi se disculpó, estaba avergonzada, se sentia

the men slept in the garage. I never knew if they were blood relatives or not, but it was obvious that they shared the poverty, the pride and their willingness to work and their nostalgia for their families and their children.

Maria, Mrs. Margiano's live-in housekeeper, was also from El Salvador. I thought that she and Noemi would get along fine. I dropped off Noemi at work in the morning. Mrs. Margiano told me that there was no need for training or translation. Maria would take care of that. I left, confident that everything would work out well.

I came back for Noemi at 4:30 in the afternoon. Mrs. Margiano opened the door. She seemed to be evasive and uncomfortable. I asked how was everything, she said OK and disappeared into the house. I was waiting outside by the garden and saw Noemi coming out of the house. Mrs. Margiano appeared at the door behind her and called out, "Stop right there!" She stopped Noemi midway between herself and me. With a satisfaction of a detective about to solve a case, she asked me in a loud and imperative voice to search Noemi's purse.

"Why? What happened?" I asked. I was not about to do what Mrs. Margiano was demanding.

"She stole perfume that cost me $100 per ounce!" she said.

Then Noemi handed me a small apparently discarded plastic bottle with some strange smelling fragrance in it. She had mixed a little bit of perfume out of three different bottles.

"The scents are ruined," Mrs. Margiano said. I offered to repay her, but she refused to accept that. Instead she wanted me to fire Noemi and never take her to work in another house in the area. I was being asked to punish this woman by denying her her livelihood.

As we got into the car, Noemi apologized. She was embarrassed, humiliated. She realized that I had the power of denying her work. Mrs. Margiano was behind me, supporting me one hundred percent. I discovered the importance of my job. I could become like a woman without a name. But I did have a name and principles and feelings. I knew that Noemi was not a thief. I gave her a lecture on the virtues of honesty, and I did my best to overcome my own embarrassment and hers. I under-

humillada. Ella sabía que yo tenía el poder temporal de dificultar su trabajo futuro. Mrs. Margiano me respaldaba totalmente. Yo descubrí la verdadera importancia de mi trabajo. Podía transformarme en una mujer sin nombre propio. Pero yo tenía nombre, sentimientos y principios propios. Yo sabía que Noemi no era una ladrona. Le dí un sermón sobre la importancia de la honestidad y la confianza en nuestro trabajo y traté de sobreponerme a nuestra vergueza mutua. Yo entendí que en manera torpe Noemi estaba tratando de llevarse prestado un poco del aroma de esa casa que parecía tener de todo y en abundancia. Ella se llevaba unas gotas del aroma de esa mágia. Noemi aprendió bruscamente que a ella sólo le correspodían las sobras descartadas de la mágia. Yo no podía agregar más castigo a la vida de Noemi. Mrs. Margiano estaba tan lejos de nosotras que no comprendía la injusticia de su demanda. Yo sí.

Noemi por propia desición buscó empleo en otra agencia. Yo continué mi tarea con una nueva conciecia sobre la importancia de mi humilde trabajo. Según mi último recuento Noemi y yo pertenecemos a la Mayoria, no a la Minoria. La Mayoria de mujeres que luchan por su independencia y trabajan por su futuro. Después de todo somos "mujeres de color" y tenemos nombres propios.

Nota:

En los estados Unidos, antes del auge del movimiento feminista, las mujeres al casarse perdían la identidad individual en público y se identificaban con el nombre y apellido del marido. Sólo usaban sus nombres propios en privado.

stood that in her mind she was not stealing. She was just borrowing a little bit of happy smell from a house that seemed to have such abundance. She wanted to take a drop or two of the magic with her. After all, Mrs. Margiano smelled so good. Noemi learned quickly that she was only entitled to the leftovers, discarded by the women without names.

I was not about to add more punishment to her life. So many things had been taken away from her already. Mrs. Margiano didn't understand. She was so far away from us. She didn't know the unfairness of her demand. I did.

Noemi went on her own accord to another agency and found another position. I continued my job with heightened consciousness. Since I counted last, I am part of the majority. So is Noemi. After all, we are women of color. And we do have names.

I Am Black, Does That Make
a Difference?

by Alane Hayes

"How was your weekend?" I asked my co-worker.

"Great! I went bowling Saturday," she said smiling.

"Oh really, I haven't gone bowling in a long time. Next time you go, let me know and I'll go with you," I said excited at the opportunity to start bowling again.

"It was really expensive," she said somewhat tentatively, "I think I'll try to find another place."

"When you decide, let me know. I'd like to go," I said again.

"Well, I'd better get back to my office," she said as she walked away down the hall, "I'll talk to you later."

A thought slowly began to take shape originating somewhere deep inside me. From there it worked its way to my consciousness. This thought was planted during my high school years when I first encountered the White world. I had refused to nurture it, so there it lay dormant—until now. Was I being rebuffed by my co-worker because I was Black?

Flashback to conversations I heard in high school:

"Did ya get all your classes?" asked Heather.

"Yea. Algebra is gonna be a lotta work though," said Shelly. "The teacher grades on a curve and there are all these Asian kids in the class. I just know they're gonna blow the curve. I can't afford to flunk this class, but I don't wanna spend all my time studying the way they do. Yuk, why are they all like that anyway?"

"Is Cindy still going out with Jim?" Karen asked.

"No. That's history," said Michelle. "She's seeing Terry now."

"Terry who?"

"God, Karen, don't you remember anybody? Terry Jackson. You know, he plays football—tall, curly black hair, dark."

"Michelle," whispered Karen, "he's Black."

"I didn't know that," said Michelle. "He doesn't look Black."
"I saw him at the mall with his mom. Michelle – he's Black."
"Oh m'god, do you think we should tell Cindy?"

My family moved to Southern California from Cleveland, Ohio when I was 16 years old. Growing up in the virtually all Black, middle class Lee-Harvard area of Cleveland, Ohio, I was not prepared for this jarring confrontation with racism. My life had been blissfully free of the racial prejudices that were experienced daily by children of other cities where there were more frequent contacts with the White population. Everywhere I went the people were Black. Riding next to me on the bus were strangers who were Black. The gentleman who owned and operated the corner store where I bought candy was Black. Growing up in a Black community, I did not think of myself as Black. There was no need to. I was not different.

My contact with White people was limited to a few teachers and the people I saw on television. The White world was not of great concern to me. I did not grow up with the attitude that their opinion of me was important. I was not taught that White people would intentionally try to interfere with my life. Yes, I heard these comments from other people but because I did not hear them in my own home, I did not believe them to be true. When planning my future, I did not feel my race needed to be a consideration.

Suddenly, in the new neighborhood and school, I was surrounded by Asians, Hispanics and the predominate White population. By bits and pieces of conversations that I heard around the campus, I realized that I would not be judged by my actions but by my color. Despite the ethnic diversity of the student population, the educational curriculum was decidedly White. In my history class in this new school, I noticed that we studied only European history. English literature covered the works by authors of English descent only. This curriculum taught "minority" students that the contributions of their cultures were not historically or artistically important enough to warrant inclusion in a text book. This was a sharp contrast to the education I received in Cleveland. There, information on Black people could be found throughout my history books.

Black people were not limited to the chapters on slavery and the civil war. I learned of the medical and political accomplishments of Blacks. I was taught that Africa had established political and educational structures long before Europe. I knew I had a heritage of which I would be proud, unlike the Black students here who learned only of their heritage during the 28 days of Black history month.

Also, I noticed that there was a sense of Black pride missing from the Black people here. They seemed to believe that their choices in life were limited to what White people would allow. This was partially fueled by the limited number of positive role models in the community and the dearth of accurate historical African and African-American information available in the schools. How can we be proud of ourselves if we only see images of slaves and savages as our ancestors? Moreover, those Blacks who have "made it" in this White society seem to have done so by patterning themselves in the model of what the Whites perceived to be "good" Blacks.

It became apparent to me that living in an integrated community, though far better than the forced segregation of the past, had its cost. The price was a loss of Black pride and loss of personal drive that is associated with it. This price can no longer be paid. The type of self-questioning that occurred after my bowling conversation is dangerous. I could have allowed it to chip away at my self-esteem by thinking that maybe I'm not equal to White people. But I refuse to think that.

I now live in a multiracial environment. I am realizing that we need to learn from each other and provide role models that have an influence on every person's life, regardless of race. In areas that house a small number of African Americans, it becomes important to network in order to instill and maintain racial self-esteem. It is also important that we as African Americans learn our own history. Without the knowledge of who we are and our history, it will be difficult to develop the strength necessary to stand against the fallacy that being African-American is a liability. This myth must be destroyed and replaced with the realization that race is a liability only when it is used as one.

A Brown Woman's Struggles

by Kanwal Yodh

Soon after our three children were in grade school, in the fall of 1970, I decided that it was time for me to look for a teaching job and put my science education to use. My husband and I had immigrated to the United States eleven years earlier. In order for my husband to find a secure position in a highly competitive job market, he had relocated several times. We were now settled in Maryland, close to Washington D.C.

Before my marriage, I had obtained a master's degree in education from the University of Chicago and also a Master of Science degree in biology from India. As a qualified science teacher, I wanted to teach young people to observe their environment, to understand their bodies, to live healthfully and to use scientific methods to solve problems. I looked forward to teaching again. Securing a teaching position in India had not been a big problem for me, and teaching science to high school students had been an enjoyable experience. Pointing out the relationship of germs to disease, studying nature's diversity, instilling a desire to learn more and using the scientific method to approach and solve problems was important to me. Housework had been minimal in India as hired help was easy to get and extended family members helped complete tasks left undone.

Having established residence in the United States, both my husband and I focused our lives on providing our American-born children with a happy, healthy and stable home environment. For twelve years I had spent my energies on being a devoted wife, mother and homemaker. I have never regretted this, but with the cost of living on the rise, I thought that a second income would help us. Yes, it was time to return to work.

In the Spring of 1971, I eagerly learned the necessary requirements to obtain recertification to teach in Maryland and in the counties near us. Visits to state and county education departments for evaluation required tedious paperwork and long drives. There was, unfortunately, no strict uniformity in the rules. Some counties required no teaching credentials and only a Bachelor's degree, while others required subject specialization for teaching.

I spent the summer updating and completing the requirements at the university for accreditation to teach science from grades 5 to 12 and sent the necessary university references and transcripts. I applied to both public and private school systems. By early summer, I had mailed thirty applications and interviewed for home instructor and substitute positions.

Much to my joy, a private school called. After a quick interview, I was promised a position in the fall. The joy was short-lived. Two days later I was informed that I was rejected because I would be unsuitable to teach the school's religion courses. This was the first blow to my pride. I rationalized that I would not have fit in that school setting anyway.

Another private school interviewer did not approve of pantsuit attire for women teachers. In fact he scrutinized my face and manner in a way that made me uncomfortable. His own manner displayed a nervousness and irritability. He said he believed that a woman and mother's place was in the home and not working outside. I tried to assure him that my attire could be changed and my household chores were organized and well taken care of. But I did not convince him. His doubts undermined my self- assurance and I felt discouraged. I wondered how he would adjust if he became disabled and his wife had to work outside.

By the end of that summer of 1971, I decided to look into non-teaching jobs. I saw that several health aide positions were available, the prerequisites for which were a motherly manner and a high school diploma. These jobs involved assisting the school nurse and keeping records.

I knew that being a health aide would not be ideal, but it was better than nothing. I applied. After the interview, I was accepted; and in the fall, I started a five and a half hour job about half-an-hour away from my home, at minimum wage ($2.54

per hour), with no benefits, in a terribly busy and rough junior high school. The regular nurse was scarcely there. Most of the time, I took care of sick and upset children. The rest of the time I completed records and called parents or rescue squads. For three years I worked at this job. I learned quickly how to handle the problems of junior high school children and how to run a place of refuge for children who wanted to get away from disagreeable classroom situations. The job had little prestige. The school administrators paid little attention to me. They viewed me as a baby sitter from the health department. It was humiliating to be treated like a non-professional. I had no input in decision-making but was loaded with the chores of the health room. I felt unappreciated

I thought of entering nursing (as nursing jobs were plentiful in those days), and I enrolled in evening classes at a junior college. This turned out to be both tiring and too expensive. Furthermore, completing this training would have required two years of clinical work. I did not want to go to school for two more years.

Teaching was still my real goal. I had kept in touch with the public school systems, updating my credits and resumé. In 1973 I was informed of three openings for qualified science teachers: two in junior high schools and one in high school. My hopes rose. However, when I went for the interviews for the junior high positions, one in Montgomery County and the other in Prince Georges County, the assistant principal told me bluntly that American children would find it hard to understand my accent. It was "foreign," he said. He was sure that parents in the neighborhood would complain about it. So, he said, perhaps I should look for another situation.

It never occurred to this educator that I was an untapped resource and might add to the children's education with my cultural background, my Indian origin and even my "exotic" accent.

Another interviewer asked me why I considered myself a better candidate, over-qualified though I was, than a fresh graduate who would cost less and be more familiar with the new curriculum. These were hard questions for me to respond to because they seemed to imply a set one. I was a square peg trying to fit into a round mold. I tried to assure him that I was willing at this point to accept the first step salary and the school system would thus be getting a well-qualified teacher for less money. I learned later that this was impossible under the laws that existed at the time.

Since then the laws have changed: public schools systems are now accepting highly qualified foreign-trained teachers at appropriate grade levels. If I were applying for those same positions today, one might suppose that I would find the system favorably disposed toward hiring me, but looking at the current selection process, I am not so sure. I notice that incoming new teachers are required to take so-called "competency tests" which means competency in taking multiple choice tests. Placing high on these tests seems more important than one's experience or previous qualifications. I feel that high scores do not necessarily make good teachers.

In my third interview, the principal of the high school discouraged me from taking the position advertised. The school was located in an unsafe area, and he implied that the safety of people coming early to work or staying late for meetings could not be guaranteed. Should incidents arise of assault or molestation, he said, the school was too understaffed to handle them. Later I learned that a male transferee was selected for the position.

At this point I felt that it would be to my advantage to explore non-teaching jobs again, so I turned to an employment agency for counseling. The experience left me more discouraged. A disinterested counselor suggested that I look into secretarial opportunities and pointed to various lists telling me to help myself.

In the spring of 1974, I took a typing course, telling myself that it would be useful even in the school system. Unfortunately, the speed tests and my lack of job references eliminated any chance of my becoming a secretary.

During the late 1970's, in the midst of the Vietnam War, there was great social upheaval which affected the student population. Those of us who lived near Washington D.C. felt the surge of the social unrest. Children reflected these changes in their behavior. They became rebellious and disenchanted. People left the area, student enrollments fell, many schools closed down. Public school systems drastically reduced their staff. Busing was tried to help create equal opportunity and to keep schools open. Some parents were angry because class sizes had suddenly bulged and diverse populations flowed into the classrooms. The climate had changed.

With the school closings, my chances of securing a position seemed remote. My applications were still on updated files, at least in my county, and it was obvious from the lack of calls that not many administrators were willing to leaf through them to take the risk of giving a chance to a person with a strange name and degrees from unknown places not easily verifiable.

This was a frustrating time for me. Our children grew, and meeting their demands took a sizeable chunk of attention after the health-aide job. My husband's work took him to conferences and national laboratories out of town. One parent needed to be at home or accessible to run the household smoothly. Although I knew that mothering was important, I could not stop yearning for a teaching job.

One evening at the end of 1974, sunshine broke through the clouds when the chairman of a high school science department called. He had gone through my files and, aware of my qualifications, was interested in interviewing me for an instructor's position. I was more than ready to leave the health room for the classroom, so I went immediately for the interview. The job consisted of assisting teachers of science in the classroom. The salary was low ($3.80/hr) and the benefits and job security meager, but I accepted and have never regretted the experience.

Perhaps these were my happiest "career" days in the United States. I worked in labs, and helped individual students as well as teachers and instructed small tutorial groups, teaching them both biology and the methods necessary to search for materials and write reports. Socially I made new friends and felt I was contributing to education in a meaningful way. Unfortunately, five years later there were more cuts and the school was closed.

I panicked! Now my chances of finding another job were even worse. I was five years older. It was August 1979. My second child was ready for college. A second income, however small, was necessary. The children had contributed towards their college funds with part-time and summer jobs. So I scanned the classified advertisements.

A small ad in the paper caught my attention for a job giving remedial help in basic science to disadvantaged youth and assisting in a learning center at the university. Quick calls, interviews, a solid background in science, and tutorial experience enabled me to secure the position. I was jubilant! Even with a low salary, inconvenient hours and a temperamental boss, it was great to be working again.

My happiness was short-lived. The following week we were informed that funds were cut and that the center would close. The boss left and the work load of the center overpowered me.

I turned to the county education department again. In late 1979-80, hiring had been frozen, but a temporary, special education, teacher's assistant position opened up. I managed to impress the interviewer because of my experience, and I relocated in a rough classroom of troubled children. I was to assist the main teacher in teaching all subjects.

Within a few weeks I became aware of the extremely difficult conditions under which the teacher worked. It was stressful to have a class of unmotivated children. There were special problems that had to be considered while teaching them. They could be rude and abusive and often time was wasted in settling them down. This was a hard challenge, but soon I felt more comfortable with these pupils. I learned to get their attention on school tasks, and I developed new working skills and new goals. I wanted to concentrate on rehabilitation and education of such children.

So when a few years later a new regional institute opened for children who were emotionally disabled learners, I wanted to be a part of this new challenging program. In the fall of 1981 I transferred to this faraway walled institute. The staff generally found it a stressful school, resulting in teacher burnout and rapid turnover. I had to develop a thick skin, listening ability and extra vision to track the troubles of these young people. With patience and persistence, I gained self-assurance and began to cultivate the extra skills used by all staff members to rehabilitate and educate above-average, disturbed youngsters. A case in point was the creativity needed to get a highly intelligent but disorganized youngster to do a focused science project, enter a county-wide competition and receive special recognition for excellence. This was no easy task. The talents of all staff members related to the student were brought into play. I felt fortunate to be part of this exciting process.

My family grew normally, with urges of teenage assertion causing pain on both sides. Now that they have outgrown rebelliousness and have matured into three responsible and caring adults, my past struggles of knocking around to get jobs as an immigrant seem like forgotten adventures. In fifteen years, I was in eight different schools. Throughout this meandering, I was fortunate to have a husband who cared, provided and shared.

In retrospect, my efforts could have been better rewarded if I had been less timid, more vocal about my needs to the "right people" and more persevering to achieve my goals. In those days, there were few support groups; equal opportunity centers and women's centers were in their infancy. Programs to update skills and day care centers for child care were even rarer.

I have few regrets. Through those years, I came to terms with reality. I was not a superwoman. I tried hard, the only way I knew to look for a science teaching job. Although I did not attain my goals exactly in the way I had envisioned, I came close and learned a great deal. Now I wish and hope to find fulfillment in helping new immigrants who have come from harder situations to find themselves in the new world.

To Auntie Nadine
With Love From Stacy

by Kelli Arakaki-Bond

Dear Auntie Nadine,

    I wish with all my heart that the blow-up in the Hana store had never happened. I detest scenes. And contrary to what you said, I truly looked forward to having a relaxing 12 days with you and the kids on Maui, Molokai, and Oahu. I do, though, think it's time that I level with you — adult to adult.

    I can understand where you're coming from when you say that you've "always been a strong person." Over the years, I've heard you and Mama talk story about growing up with Grandma. You two enjoyed the way she'd round up all the kids in your Honakaa neighborhood to produce stick dancing and hula shows. Both of you loved the way she could belt out the Hawaiian National Anthem at the same time she'd pluck that ukelele or pound those piano keys.

    But you said you and Mama used to cry when Grandma would vanish for hours. She wasn't lifting her glorious mezzo-soprano or putting on some pageant to benefit the church, you recalled. She'd be partying at someone's house — too wired on sloe gin or vodka to give a damn about coming home to make supper for you and Mama. Grandma would scare you, I remember you saying. One moment she'd be all tickles and kisses. Then, quicker than a lava flow, she'd use on you whatever object was handy at the moment.

    She'd be too bombed, you continued, to know what she was doing when she fled to the beds of other men. You said she did this following the often bloody fights she and your stepdad would start with each other after a few nips. He would often turn his fists on you and Mama, you mentioned, and Grandma was too drunk most times to stop him.

    Once again, I completely understand your pleas to accept

you for yourself — especially with all that you put up with. You've had to be strong to survive all that, plus your marriage. A relationship with another alcoholic—one who has been writing the same book for the last 25 years and who has disappeared for hours while struggling to move to new residences — has got to be hell. Your jobs as an assistant hospital administrator, a mother of four teenagers and a household manager are no paradise, either.

What's not o.k., though, is how your need for control pervades everything you do. You and I have always gotten along well — up until now. I've concluded that our "harmony" existed as long as I've played the compliant child.

I tried to tell you what bothered me hours before our fight in the store. What irked me was the way you told me to turn up the air conditioning. When I merely suggested that the house was already chilly and that everyone went scrambling for a sweater. You barked, "DO AS I TELL YOU!" I was humiliated, especially when you snapped your command in front of a room full of teenagers and I'm 23 years old. Then when I scolded the little ones for climbing the couch, you snickered, "Don't philosophize."

After we fought in the market, you wasted no time in painting yourself as the eternal martyr, elevating yourself while dismissing me as an ungrateful brat. You even downed three bottles of wine that night with your Auntie Regina. Then you berated me for not taking responsibility.

Look who's talking! If you're asking to renew our relationship on the old terms, I can't do it and still feel good about myself.

I want to know you better, Auntie. I don't know what's going on with you on the inside. Almost everything I hear about your life comes from Mama, who seems to have overcome the wretched childhood you and she endured. I notice you've resorted to the "don't philosophize" routine in the last five years when I've offered my insights and feelings on "adult" (read: emotionally loaded) topics.

When you say that, I feel like I've trod on raw nerves. It tells me how vulnerable you are beneath all that "take-charge" armor. Yet you want me to understand you completely. How can I do that without mind-reading, a skill I fail miserably at? And wasn't it you who told me to speak my mind when I was a shy 13-year-old?

Auntie, I want our relationship to change. Obedience served its purpose when I was little. Today, however, I feel that the only way I can relate to my elders is from a position of mutual respect. It's one thing to uphold our cultural heritage. But it's another when honor of older people turns into fear. Our family has taken the old Hawaiian way of relating too far. They've used tradition as an excuse to maintain the grogginess they've lived in for five generations.

You and I have a chance to transcend that.

With love,

Stacy

POEMS

盆

周 麗 珍 原作
廖 茂 俊 譯

給 大 姨，1909－1987

我們站在這兒，
獻上祭品，清水，紙錢，壽衣，
拜別離我們而去的靈魂。
在街坊燒衣。

我們站在這兒，
靜靜的獻上
腌肉，泡菜，齊食，
和一碗覆滿温瓜的白飯。

我們站在這兒，
兩旁佈滿粉紅包肉紙的小巷，
喪宴就在俱樂部後，
一個充斥塵土的停車場裡。

我們站在這兒，
和每個致哀者，
等着您，大姨！
等着無休止的喪禮開始。
現在我真的意識到的是，
一年後，反覆再反覆的練習。

POON

For Di Yee, 1908-1987

We stand with food
water for washing
money and clothing for
the souls of our departed
Gai Fong Shieu Yee
the community clothes burning

We stand
quietly beside tins layered with
salt pork, pickled vegetables,
jzai, and steaming rice topped
with wedges of warm watermelon

We stand
beside tins placed evenly
along two sides of pink butcher paper
stretched down the alley
a banquet on the dirt
in the dry, dusty parking lot
behind the club

We stand
two participants among many
each at our places waiting
You, Di Yee, beside me
Awaiting the start of
the timeless ritual
the importance I only sense now
after years of repeated practice
repeated

我們站在這兒，
靠近脚旁有一盆水，
一條新毛巾，
正等着被用來擦拭。
折疊式的桌子緊壓着粉紅包肉紙。

我們站在這兒，
背對着被杯子圍着的一盤豬頭，
酒杯整齊的排列着，
覆滿瓜皮的白飯正等着用來致祭。

我們站在這兒，
被一種無形的時間光束，
牽引到這兒，
等待喪禮的開始。
距離與希望將我們從子宮中抽出。
然後，重覆的在這兒廻旋。
在巷裡，
在塵埃中，
在夜裡。

我們站在這兒，
等待着死者來食。
　　只聽大姨説：
　　" 端起盆！毛巾！倒掉水！"
　　我趕忙回答：
　　" 我會的！我會的！"

We stand
maneuvered by you near the foot
where the basin of water
and the new towel wait to serve
on the folding table
holding down this end of the
long stretch of pink butcher paper

We stand
opposite the head
where the pig head sits plattered
trapped between cups of tea
lined in some order
cups of wine lined
in some order
bowls of rice
wedges of watermelon
lined
waiting to serve

We stand
all of us drawn here
by an invisible cord eons long
awaiting the start of a ritual
removed from its womb
by distance and by hope
and repeated here
in the alley
in the dirt
in the evening
We stand waiting to feed the dead

> *"Get the poon! And the towel!*
> *Pour the water out first!"*
> *You, Di Yee, say*
> *"I will, I will."*
> *I answer*

盆，
一個新的錫盆，
我們用它洗淨自己後，
再用毛巾擦乾。

爲了確保健康而洗滌，
在鬼魂洗滌的地方洗滌。
在鬼魂洗了之後，
用他們剩餘的水洗滌。

我靜靜的站在這兒，
等待着一陣微風，空氣，和
一種莫名的訊號。
然而，
他們却悄悄的以無形的雙手，
摸索他們的佳餚，
飽餐一頓他們的美味。

一刹那之間，
一連串華麗的屁，
驅使所有致哀的人，
將逝者吃剩的食物，
一盤，兩盤，三盤···的吃完。

　我彷彿還聽見大姨説着：
　“　端起盆來！”
　明年還會再説：
　“　先倒掉水！”

The poon
the new tin basin
from which we later wash ourselves
and the towel
on which we will later dry

We will wash to insure health
Wash where the ghosts have washed
before us
Wash after ghost have washed
Wash in their leftovers

I stand quietly
awaiting a breeze, a gust of air,
some kind of signal
but they come silently
invisible hands groping at the best,
eating the choicest

Suddenly a flourish of motion
live participants bend
and gather the food tins
one, two, three or more
leftovers from the dead
for the living to eat.

> *"Get the poon!"*
> *I can still hear you, Di Yee,*
> *And you'll say again next year*
> *"Dump the water out first!"*

當我等待時，
給我指示，
刷子對着我，
讓游動的風煽起塵埃來。
在我端起您遺留的盆，毛巾時，
來些笑話吧！

As I wait
give me a sign
brush against me
shuffle the wind
stir the dust
say something funny
before I get the poon
and the towel
and wash
in your leftovers.

Janet Jue

阿　婆

周　麗　珍　原作

廖　茂　俊　譯

阿婆！
您可曾知道‧‧‧‧‧
您出殯那天下雪了？
四十年來，
我從不曾見過這樣的雪！
雪，
在轉瞬間溶化了，消失了‧‧‧
　　黛絲姨在車上說着話，
　　我們依偎在雪佛蘭的車座後，
　　大衣纏結着我們，
　　雙臂緊緊壓着肋骨，
　　兩肘緊緊頂着胃，
　　手提包平躺在合攏的雙膝上。
車停了，
我循着新雪的痕跡，
裹了個雪球擲向了喬埃。
穿着暗藍色西服的喬埃，
突感受了這個莫名的舉措。
起初，
每人面色凝重，
而後，
周太太來了，
接着是愛迪思，
再接着是，

　　三個穿着
　　寬腿褲，
　　平底鞋，
　　廉價手織開襟毛衣，
　　嘴上喋喋不休的阿姨們。
吵雜聲直到儀式開始，
吵雜聲直到過了十二點，
過了十二點半，
過了十二點三刻。
一切只為了牧師能等待便多
因天氣影響而遲來的致哀者。

AH POAH

Do you know that it snowed
on the day of your funeral, Ah Poah?

"I've never seen it snow like this
        in forty years!
The last time it melted right away —
        didn't stay
Melted and didn't stay—
Snow"
        Auntie Daisy said as we rode
        cramped in the back seat of the Chevy
        coats tangled stuffing us
        arms tight pressed against our ribs
        elbows jabbed into our stomachs
        purses balanced on our closed knees

When we stopped I tracked new fallen snow
Scooped a ball and threw at Joe
        at Joe
        in his dark blue suit
        who felt the act inappropriate

Everyone was solemn at first
Then Mrs. Chow arrived
Then Edith
And with Auntie, the three chattered and yakked
        in their wide leg pants, flat shoes and
        self-knit cardigans of sale yarn
Chattered until the service started
Chattered until past twelve
        past twelve thirty
        past twelve forty-five
        as the minister waited for more mourners
        because of the weather he surmised aloud

吵雜聲是為寧靜的恐懼
而吵雜。
當我抓住塑膠購物袋的把手時，
霎時間，奶油糖掉落了下來，
甜香味驅走了悲傷，
剩余的綑裝五分錢，
足以買更多的甜香。

當他開始讀到您時，
阿婆！
您是一個平凡的人，
在您樸實的一生中，
您是一個母親，
一個家庭主婦，
一個園丁，
一個守了二十一年的寡婦。
讀到這裡，
想想啊！　好一個平凡的人！

在下着雪的二月四日，
冷風吹進了教堂裡，
擦亮了長檯，也清淨了贊美詩集。
合唱團在您生命中，
唱出了 " 奇妙的恩典 "
"　周安樂！"
他從本子上念出了這個名字。
"　愛她的花園！"

三十五年來，不曾用過美國名字。
三十五年來，不曾說過一個複合句。
不管您用我給你的鵝媽媽辭典(從A到Z)
做了些什麼？

他提到，您將您的一生貢獻給了家人，
撫育您的兒子，
將您的樂趣种植在您的花園，
老來含飴弄孫。

Chattered for fear of silence
Chattered
While I clutched the handles of the plastic grocery bag
    that rustled full of butterscotch drops—
    sweets to the mourners to chase away the sadness—
    and white wrapped nickels
    to buy more sweets

When he began to read that you, Ah Poah,were
    an ordinary person
A humble one whose life was one of being a mother
    homemaker
    gardener
Widowed for twenty-one years, he read
Think of it! An ordinary person!

Chill air filled the room of scarless polished pews
    and clean hymnals
    on February 4th as it snowed

The taped choir sang "Amazing Grace" between
    your life's interludes
"Chow On Lok,"he read from his notes
    "loved her garden"

    No American name in thirty-five years!
    Not one compound sentence in thirty-five years!
    Whatever did you do with the Mother Goose Dictionary
    (Apple to Zebra) I gave you?

He read yours was a life devoted to your family
    spent nurturing your son
Your pleasure was in your garden, he read
And caring for your son
And playing with your grandson

阿婆！
您的那些熱情，熱誠呢？
您那常穿着到處走動的
自己縫的褲子和廉價花上衣呢？
您在厨房和院子以前的歲月呢？
在鹵味火雞，煎堆，和芝麻餅以前呢？
在您又熱的厨房裡，
爲您在美國生的家人，
油炸您剛殺的肥油雞以前呢？
除了您雙手把＂冬瓜＂，＂蘭豆＂，
＂絲瓜＂，＂豆角＂，＂佛瓜＂
懸掛在蒼翠繁茂的籬笆上以外的事呢？

阿婆！
有誰知您擔任過什麼角色？
您又告訴了誰？
什麼是您的初戀？
是那位輕撫您的頭的叔叔？
是祖母笑呵呵的答應了您？
是那位在新年給您＂利是＂買甜食的人？
誰爲您做＂芝麻餅＂，＂煎堆＂？
爲您縫衣服？
爲您扎辮子？
您現在枕着的白緞枕頭，
可就是您的第一個？

Ah Poah, what about your other passions
Other zeals?
Of time before toddling and
shuffling around in home-sewn pants
and cheap flowered blouses?
Of your years before the kitchen and yard?
Before "noa mai" stuffed turkeys, "gyn due,"
and "gee ma beng?"
Before the fat, juicy chickens you butchered
and fried in your small, hot kitchen
for your American born family"?
Beyond "dong gwa," "lon dow," "sing gwa,"
"dow gakwk," bok choy,"
and "foo gwa" draped and hanging
lush and thick over trellises wired together
by your hands?

Ah Poah, who knows where you played?
Who did you tell?
What of your first love?
The uncle who patted your head?
The grandmother who clucked approval at you?
The ones who gave you "lai she" to buy sweets
on New Year's Day?
Who made your "gee ma beng?"
Your "gyn dui?"
Sewed your dresses?
Braided your hair?
The white satin pillow your head now rests on—
is it your first?

牧師説：" 這一章，是結束了！"
　　" 可是，書却没有完結！"

當他閔上了書。
一切都結束了。
或許當您的護柩者，
蹣跚的走在雪地上。
將您的頭轉向您希望的假湖，
就在二月四日下雪前‥‥
您從挨家推銷的推銷員那兒
買來計謀的那天。

　阿婆，
　您並没有選擇了睡眠，
　而是我們其他的人選擇了它，
　我們有些人已經在那兒買了牀。
　爲什麽？
　爲什麽您選擇了一個離每個人，
　那麽遥遠的地方？

"This chapter," the minister said, "is finished."
"But," he consoled, "the book is not."

It closed.
It closed when he closed the lid.
Or, maybe when your pallbearers
stumbling in the snow
turned your head to the fake lake as you'd wished
at the plot you bought from the door-to-door salesman—
before it snowed on February 4th in Bakersfield, California.

Ah Poah, you didn't choose to sleep
where the rest of our folks are
Where some of us have already bought a bed.
Why?
What made you choose a place so
far from everyone
else?

Janet Jue

大きな入植地の家

サリー・サチエ・ヒルケマ

大きな農場の家は　丘の上に建っていた
化け物じみたアメリカねむの木に覆われて
蔓が枝枝への梯子のように　垂れ下がり
轟々と音立てる流れに接した谷に抱かれて
そこは　静かな場所だった
やかましい九官鳥たちだけが沈黙を破り
農場の家は　十人の日本人家族を守った
そこはまだ　とても淋しい場所だった

家の中は押し殺した声とささやきだけ
ああ　それがあたりまえの話し方だった
おしゃべりは　古い木製ラジオから流れ
わたしたちはほんのわずかの言葉を　飲み込みさえした
祖父が食べ物を噛む音だけが聞こえそうで
入れ歯がカチカチ鳴るのを聞いた
わたしは覚えている
食卓でやかましく揺らすわたしの椅子を
祖父にフォークで小突かれたのを

風呂場は母屋から離れていて
大きな木の浴槽を囲む壁は
脚長ぐもが巣をかける棲み家だった
恐ろしいごきぶりたちが　強靭な羽をばたつかせ
家族は　強引にからだをごしごし擦った
ごきぶりたちを　熱い浴槽に沈め
どんな表情も感情も捨てて　溺死させ
わたしたちは沈黙のうちに沈黙を重ねた

（訳／しま・ようこ）

THE PLANTATION HOUSE

The large plantation house sat on a low hill
Covered with monstrous monkey-pod trees
Vines hanging like ladders to their branches
Nestled in a valley bordered by the rumbling stream
And it was a quiet place
Only loud mynah birds interrupted the silence
The house held a Japanese family of ten
Still it was a lonely place.

Inside the house was a hush and a whisper
Oh, there was the normal talk
And the chatter from the old wooden radio
We even ate without too many words
Only grandpa's chewing seemed to be heard
I could hear the click of his false teeth
I remember being poked with a fork
For noisily tilting my chair at the table.

The bath house was separate from the main house
The walls that surrounded the stained wooden hot tub
Was home to leggy spiders that built their webs
Menacing cockroaches fluttered with strong wings
The family scrubbed their bodies vigorously
And submerged them in the steaming water
Drowning any expression or feelings left
We became silent over our silence.

Sarie Sachie Hylkema

傷つきやすいわたし

サリー・サチエ・ヒルケマ

どうしてわたしは　こんなにおどおどしているの
つけねらわれた　子鹿のように
彼女が静かにくつろいで
クロッカスをそっと覗きながら牧草の中へ入って行くと
両耳をそば立てる
仲間の　沈黙の急襲を聞きつけたかのように
彼女のそばにいると
それが　わたしの内側を傷つける
痛手を負ったわたしだから？

そう　わたしはまたしても傷ついてしまう
傷あとはまだ癒されないまま
過ぎ去った愛の出会いから
突然消えてしまった男への愛まで
神は　何かしらわたしに予告する
身に纏ったいばらの激情で
神の頬に涙が伝い
手のひらの傷を見るとき
わたしの中の　やさしい心が蘇る

（訳／しま・ようこ）

THE FRAGILE ME

Why do I feel so fragile
Like a spotted fawn
As she quietly eases herself
Into the meadow with crocuses peeking
Ears alert as if to hear
The quivering rush of her mate
To be by her side
Is this the wounded me?

It hurts inside of me

Yes, I feel fragile again
The scars still not healed
From past encounters with the living
To have loved a man and then not
My God anoints me somehow
With the passion of wearing thorns
And as I see the tear on his cheek
The stain on his palm
I remember the humanness in me.

Sarie Sachie Hylkema

日本の娘

サリー・サチエ・ヒルケマ

娘は　注意深く歩く
雑草が芽吹く歩道を
黄色い皮膚の下を見つめながら
絹の結び目のおさげ髪を
ゴムバンドとリボンで結び
まっすぐに切りそろえた前髪
母がていねいにプレスしてくれた
のりがきいて　ぱりっとした服
まっ白に磨かれたテニスシューズ
くるぶしで二つ折りしたソックス
切り抜きの　紙人形
庭の木にたてつくすべも知らない
泥だらけの飼い犬を抱いて
あなたは　汚れなく純粋でなくては
これが　日本の娘のあるべき姿
清潔で　きびきびと　手垢のつかないままで

（訳／しま・ようこ）

JAPANESE GIRL

The girl walks cautiously down
The sidewalk with weeds pushing up
Seeing the undersides of yellow skin
Her hair braided like silk knots
Tied with rubber bands and ribbon
Bangs straight, cut from a bowl
Dress starched and ironed crisp
Pressed neatly by her mother
Tennis shoes polished white
Socks folded in half at the ankles
A cut-out paper doll
Do not lean against the tree in the yard
Or hug the dirty family dog
You must be pure, unsoiled
That is how Japanese girls should look
Clean, crisp, untouched and unused.

Sarie Sachie Hylkema

LIKE MY FATHER

He does not look like my father
His tall frame commands like
Eucalyptus trees on the Kula meadows
Silver hair covers a prominent face
Eyes that flow in from the ocean
Marine green of Kapalua Bay
Skin is color of parchment paper
Speckled with aging spots
Scarred with the battles of youth
He is a white man; my father is Asian.

He is quiet like my father
I only feel his body in the house
There is barely an utter in his room
A mystery novel without a clue
Walls quickly put up to keep out secrets
Closed to the chatter of the living
The demanding cries of loved ones
A monk in hushed faded robe
Denying the talking people to respond
As we succumb to the law of his silence.

I watch him from a distance
Wondering if he will let me inside
To let me soothe his pain
Or somehow quell his anger
But again it is not the time
Not the time to intrude
Maybe tomorrow his inner child
Will let him come and play with me
He is helplessly Asian
Like my father.

Unlike my father
He learned later
That he had intelligence
School, books and teachings fascinated him
Like the young boy with his chemistry set
No longer did his normal idle play
Seem enough to hold him
He is in awe of his accomplishments
A college education, courageous pursuits
As he ages.

LIKE MY FATHER, he believes in God
There is intense integrity and compassion
UNLIKE MY FATHER, he comes from the street
I love them both.

Sarie Sachie Hylkema

STRAWBERRIES

An unlikely topic
As I weave in and out
Of consciousness
A set of eight needles
Tiny prickles
Gently placed between my eyes
On my wrists and feet
A Chinese acupuncturist
Who disclaims my fear
Says it is menopause
Lack of red blood
Brings me back to my
Strawberries.

Strawberries
Between my teeth
I feel the fuzz of skin, I bite
The juice squirts on my tongue
Taste buds delight
I remember the tartness
Of last night
The late hour, passion
Loving a man
Succumbing to the heart
He loves me differently
Like I love strawberries

Strawberries
"I'll taste your strawberries
I'll drink your sweet wine"
A lyric soothes from a radio
Finding a spot inside of me
To remember that
I live in the today
Not the yesterday or tomorrow
Letting go of fear
Embracing the living
and I'll savor
The strawberries.

Sarie Sachie Hylkema

CHOCOLATE CHIP ICE CREAM

Eating chocolate chip ice cream

I am sitting
At the counter at Lahaina Drugs
Sipping a 25 cents chocolate coke
Straw that sucks thick syrup
From the bottom of the glass
Bittersweet.

The Japanese man behind the soda fountain
In pointed white cap
Asks, "How was school today?"
Did he really want to know
Or was he just passing the humid day
Dreaming of leaving the islands
A romance with a woman
Skin ivory and hair blonde?

I scan the magazine stand
For a new movie magazine
Jeffery Hunter smiles back at me
It's time to go
Down the dusty dirt road that leads
To my house on the sand
My mother greets me
"Do you have any homework?"

Eating chocolate chip ice cream
Back to my childhood days
The taste is the same
And so am I.

Sarie Sachie Hylkema

"Writing is an act of hope."

Isabel Allende

CHANCE

1
Solitude comes to sit by my side
it settles down for a long stay
and I am at a loss for words

2
Intervals
and the final moment.
Later I will contemplate the changes
in a port city.
It is better to read in your eyes
than to leave.

3
I went like the wind.
I left delay behind.
Because I arrived running.
Because the journey has not begun.

4
I look at my photos,
I'm not the same.
Nor am I the same in the mirror.

Because the circle is closing.

5
I was small
a guest of all the rivers
I have changed little.

Nature has managed everything
on time.

Casualidad No Es Una Mujer

1

La soledad se pone a mi lado,
se acomoda para mucho tiempo
y yo no sé qué decir.

2

Intervalos
y el final.
Más tarde contemplaré los cambios
en un puerto.
Sería mejor leer en los ojos
que partir.

3

Fuí como nada.
Dejé el retraso.
Porque llegué corriendo.
Porque el viaje aún no ha comenzado.

4

Observo mis fotografías,
no soy la misma.
No soy la misma tampoco en el espejo.

Porque ahora el círculo se cierra.

5

Yo era pequeña,
era huesped de todos los ríos
y he cambiado muy poco.

La naturaleza lo hizo todo
a tiempo.

6

I am troubled by this woman
who feels
that objects, furniture are unaware.
Who feels
that she moves beyond bricks and mortar
to the sky's silences.

7

Destiny is like an oven
like a dark, oppressive heat
like fear.

I am troubled by this woman
who for a long time now
has taken me by her hand
so that we may seek
a place to be born.

8

But she doesn't want to leave.
She says the chosen place is sufficient
that misery is also elsewhere
and that despair is the only certainty

She wants to know
how many years have passed.

9

My house.
My house is empty
and the photographs speak all at once.

She has left.
I feel I didn't send away her
that I wanted to know.

6

Me duele esta mujer
la que siente
que los muebles ignoran.
La que siente
que se traslada a través de los ladrillos
a los silencios del cielo.

7

El destino es igual que un horno,
que un calor oscuro,
que el miedo.

Me duele esta mujer
que hace mucho tiempo
me tomó de la mano
para que buscáramos
un lugar para nacer.

8

Pero ella no quiere partir.
Dice que el lugar elegido es bueno.
Que la basura está fuera
y que nada es mas seguro que la desesperación.

Se esfuerza por saber
cuantos años pasaron.

9

Mi casa.
Vacío mi casa
y las fotografías hablan todas a la vez.

Ella se fue.
Siento que no despedí
a quien quería conocer.

10
I suspect
that ineluctably
time is drifting away.
Since I have come from everywhere.

I must carry faith
hanging around my neck
like a God's image.
Maybe I'll discover it.

11
I can't remember
how many times I've seen myself.
I only know that I almost froze
facing my image.

Perhaps I am enamored
of my search.

12
Silence.
Look at me.
Love me,
and let music kiss me
since grief always awaits.
know it isn't always
necessary to be strong.

13
Avarice isn't always tolerable
and "casualidad" is not a woman.

If it were thus
then don't regale me with flowers
and every day I hear the imploring
voice of the other
that I bear within me.

10
Sospecho
que inquebrantablemente
el tiempo se va.
Como me fuí yendo de todas las partes.

He de llevar la fe
colgada
como la imagen de un Dios.
Tal vez lo encuentre.

11
No puedo recordar
las veces que me he visto.
Sólo puedo saber
qûe casi me quedo mirándome.

Tal vez esté enamorada
de mi búsqueda.

12
Silencio
Mírame
Amame
Y deja que la música me bese,
que el dolor siempre espera.
Ya sé que a veces
no es necesario ser fuerte.

13
No siempre se puede tolerar la avaricia,
Y la casualidad no es una mujer.

Si así fuera,
que no se me den flores,
que todos los días oigo implorante
la voz de otra que llevo dentro.

14
I looked at silence
and asked myself
if it would like to pierce me
as when it was part of a dream.

And I asked why
I don't want to shield myself
from its affection.

15
My reality
doesn't reach the garden

I'll play the same game to the end;
till I remember
that I have no right
to be my own victim

16
I baptized my tongue
with a soft murmur,
and played the last note.

I would like to weep
as when questions
were not urgent.

17
I would like to know
which is the best way
and what its meaning.

I would like to bite
to nourish myself.
To feel the glance burst forth.
To know there is blood.

14
Miré el silencio
y me pregunté
si le gustaría penetrarme
como cuando era parte de un sueño.

Y me pregunté, por qué
no quiero defenderme de su cariño.

15
Mi realidad
no llega hasta el jardín.

Jugaré hasta el final,
hasta recordarme
que no tengo derecho
de ser mi propia víctima.

16
Bauticé mi lengua
con un lento zumbido,
y toqué la última nota.

Me gustaría llorar
como cuando las preguntas
no tenían apuro.

17
Me gustaría saber
cuál es la mejor manera
y cuál el sentido que debo darle.

Me gustaría morder
alimentarme.
Sentir que la mirada brota.
Saber que hay sangre.

18
To go out into the world
although it seems merciless

To make silences bleed
with cries of alarm,
and agitate the birds of the forest.

19
Hell dwells within me
lives, walks in me.
I live with the silent cries of fear.

As with everyone:
the Hell I have created.

20
I was confident
and began the monologue.

I told myself nothing
has happened.
I have my roses.

Florinda Mintz

Translated by Julian Palley

18
Salir al mundo
aunque parezca despiadado.

Hacer sangrar los silencios
con todos los gritos,
y agitar las aves del bosque.

19
El infierno me camina dentro,
vive conmigo.
Vivo con los silenciosos gritos del miedo.

Como todos,
mi propio infierno.

20
Tuve confianza
y comencé el monólogo.

Me dije que nada ha pasado.
Tengo mis rosas.

Florinda Mintz

Versión Original
Veinte poemas cortos esritos
entre 1980 y 1984 en Buenos Aires
y California

RELATIONSHIPS

Relationships s t r e t c h
settle down
are dissolved
find themselves
venerated
are destroyed
are repeated
seek one another
love each other
disappear
are denuded
love each other
are frightened
torture each other
surrender

are revealed

Florinda Mintz

Translated by Julian Palley

RELATIONSHIPS

Las relaciones se estiran

se acomodan

se desuelven

se veneran

se destrozan

se repiten

se buscan

se quieren

se desvanecen

se desnudan

se aman

se asustan

se torturan

se entregan

Florinda Mintz

Vertical

to Robert Juarroz

Under the infinite dome
each speaks to himself
distancing that which
is secret and ferocious

In the corner of circumstance
I move from silence
to ecstasy

I limit the distances
the instants of those storms
that smash us like a grenade
tossed against a wall

to speak to oneself
tranquilizes
convinces

is like walking in reverse
and repeating oneself
                    backwards
and frontwards

Florinda Mintz

Translated by Julian Palley

VERTICAL

a Roberto Juarroz

Bajo la boveda infinita
cada uno habla consigo mismo
retirando fuera aquello
secreto y feróz

en la esquina de las circunstancias
transcurro del silencio
al éxtasis

limito las distancias
los instantes de esas tempestades
que nos destroza como una granada
arrojada contra la pared

hablar consigo mismo
tranquiliza
convence

es como caminar hacia atrás
y repetirse al revés
        y al derecho

Florinda Mintz

わたしの故郷、この地球

やまだ・みつえ

想い描いてみよう　未来のあることを
土星の環のように　わたしたちを結ぶ
平和のかたい輪
戦争のための空間など　ありはしない

想い描いてみよう　未来のあることを
わたしの故郷
この地球に
核戦争の
実験場など　もうありはしない

想い描いてみよう　未来のあることを
わたしたちの魂のガイガーカウンター
カチカチ音立てる悪夢を　とらえたりしない

そこには
炭のかけらのように
焼かれ　大地に埋められた
母の姿を見る子どもは
もういない。

そこには
戦争に殺された
戦場で殺された
憎しみに殺された
飢えに殺された
子どもたちの柩に突っ伏して
泣き叫ぶ母は
もういない

My Home Town This Earth

Imagine there is a future
where a tight ring of peace
like Saturn's collar
holds us all in
and there is no
space for war

Imagine there is a future
where my home town
this earth
is no longer
an experimental station
for nuclear wars

Imagine there is a future
where our psychic Geiger counters find
no clicking nightmares in the air

Where no child
sees its mother's image
in pieces of charcoal
buried in the ground
where she was burned

where no mother cries
over her child's coffin
killed at war
killed in the war
killed by hate
killed by hunger

わたしは　老いていくからだを横たえる
わたしたちの共有の未来と
分け合った過去の　交わる地点へ
四肢を広げて
そして　心に刻み込もう

未来は確かにあることを
生きのびるだけでは　決して満足しない人びとにも
死と滅亡さえ恐れない人びとにも
そしてまた
そこに未来があると　胸に描けない不具の人びとにも
未来は確かにあることを
そういう彼ら彼女らにも
未来は　あるに違いないことを

そしてまた　想い描いてみよう
誤った見方で
ここで　わたしたちを監視し
いま　わたしたちを見張っている
そんな眼にも　未来のあることを

（訳／しま・ようこ）

I lay my aging woman body
on this ground
spread eagled
reaching to four points
of our common future
our shared pasts
and remember

we must make a future
for those for whom survival only
is not enough
we must make a future
for those so bereft in mind and spirit
they cannot imagine there is a future.

Imagine there is a future
for eyes
watching us here
watching us now
through the wrong end of a telescope.

Mitsuye Yamada

FOR PRISCILLA

During the years you were in China we led undirected lives
until you sent us each disjointed sentences on strips of paper
and steered us together by remote control
while we read your jig-sawed letter.

Last Easter you brought my first experience of the Passover Seder
because, you said, I mustn't spend my Easter sick in bed.
You brought into my dining room the shankbone, roasted egg,
bitter-herbs, and turkey, basted, broiled, and spiced.
You marched in with your own team of out-of-town guests
and conducted our recitation from Ben Shahn's Haggadah.

Now night has fallen on the lids of your home on the hill
and on the ferns of hair in your walkway.
Strange heels clatter against the blue and white tiles
you laid on your floors with rubber-gloved hands, and
the black angry streak you marked on Laguna Canyon Road
is now muted by more drunken tires.

How shall we now celebrate next year's Easter/Passover
without your own homey brand of the Seder Table?
We will count the number of chairs around our table
...again and again.
Pockets of air will not be filled
with the warm shrill of your voice.

But Priscilla
the tracks you left with your poems will stay
to press my ears with your laughter and
now I must grow old for the both of us.

Mitsuye Yamada

FILLING THE BLANKS

Memories are sold every day
at the mortuary chain
your family felt forced to choose.
Four grand buys the standard package,
all the makings
of a do-it-yourself funeral kit.
The fake marble jewel case
exhibits one's body,
a rainbow wax curio
polished to trigger
the correct face-to-handkerchief burials
and varnished to stall decay
in the concrete-coated underground.
An extra eight hundred bucks
lets the departed one go skeleton
in Ortho Posturepedic comfort.
The family booth stands
with its springform theatre seats
and black drapes
that open to pre-taped organ chords
originally recorded
for an amusement park haunted house.
Over this, a custom-recited
fill-in-the-blank eulogy:
birthdate, birthplace, names of survivors.
Education, occupation and hobbies
optional for female decedents.

Salespeople lurked
waiting to descend on your family's tears,
the perfect opportunity
to peddle the house clergyman's
monotone recital of Scripture.

At your memorial
I would wait for him to complete
the empty spaces
on your tribute form.
I could have given him
twenty years of commentary
starting with your move next door
on the brink of the Watts Riots,
no high school diploma,
the only working mom on the block then.
You snapped your back
over coffee shop tables
and over the floors and toilets
in other people's homes
to keep hubby's own barbershop open,
and defended your boy
from neighborhood finks
even at age 19
when he crippled my sheltie
with a b-b gun.
Aprons, brushes, timeclocks and alibis
later bowed to your reign
as full-time queen of the home party
Shaklee, Tupperware, Amway.
Princess House, Sarah Coventry.
These ventures won you trips
to Las Vegas, Omaha, Anchorage.
Between coffee table gatherings and vacations
you turned egg cartons and broken glass
into swag lampshades I coveted.
You whipped a laundry beach bottle
and dry cleaner plastic
into an Easter bunny basket
I adored so much
that the pipecleaner fuzz
disappeared from the ears.

During all this, the cigarettes
leading to the cobalt,
the hairlessness,
the retching before and after the meals
you continued to make
while hubby glazed in front of the pay t.v.
and eyeballed the next door widow-to-be.

Twenty years of stories
and the minister summoned neither me
nor anyone else
to the pulpit.
My jaws clenched.
Two people restrained me in my seat
as he tallied—into the microphone —
your two daughters
three sons
five stepsons
nine grandchildren
for the sum of good wife and mother.

Kelli Arakaki-Bond

MIDNIGHT SUPPER PARTY

I was made
of rainbow ribbons
streaming from the mouths
of five different women
locking hands and singing
at a midnight supper party

Kwan Yin
merciful Chinese Mother
straddled a dolphin
on the Northeastern Sea
to start this affair
my conception

Other creatures
aided Kwan Yin.
The serpent carried water.
The tiger gathered firewood.
The peacock dusted the deck
with her feathers
pulling pea pods
coriander
bok choy
stirred in the soup
by goddess Pele
rising from the flames
hugging the cauldron

Pele
brought brandy,
the awa drink
of old Hawaii
festooned the table
with guavas and bananas
abalone shells

Kwan Yin and Pele
invited Cailleach
from the forests
of Scotland and Ireland
leeks and potatoes strapped
her eagle back
picking up Fedelm
English poetess
and Ukemochi
matriarch of rice
seaweed and virgin tuna
from Japan

They all feasted
under a purple canopy
appliqued by the full moon
lighting the path
for my creation
with the million lanterns
of Fedelm's words:
> *"After our meal*
> *let your throats receive*
> *a squishy squiggle*
> *issue strips of color*
> *you will want to braid*
> *into a baby girl*
> *future bard*
> *abacus woman*
> *protector of females*
> *hearthkeeper*
> *gowned in 24 karat gold.*
> *Do it now!"*

At that urging, the women
of the midnight supper party
laced their voices
and ate silkworms
for dessert.

Kelli Arakaki-Bond

LUNCHTIME AT THE SANTA ANA DMV

California: 24K POET
my license plate
forbids me to slip unnoticed
past hamburger stand drive-up windows
let alone the car registration line
at the Santa Ana DMV.
The clerk asked me
grill him a poem
and my microwave mouth
refrained from flashing
that custom-ground and cut
USDA Prime verses
take longer to cook
than a Big Mac
Jumbo Jack
Happy Star
Whopper charred.
So, I fried up
a bag of writer's block
grabbed my sticker
and hightailed it
to the nearest McDonald's!

Kelli Arakaki-Bond

CORNUCOPIA

You unwind your hose in my garden,
that thirsty triangle of dark earth.
Specks gather deep in two circles.
The pindots leave one at a time,
catch beads from your spray
to rest along my humus.
Angel hair anchors the slumbering seeds.

They awaken, shells cracking.
The growth thickens from their bases.
New hanger-rod roots bend underground.
Shoots emerge from my plot.
Some greet the sun in greens and golds.
Others meet daylight in shades of brown.

They develop into crops and trees,
expand my patch to an open field
irrigated by your reservoir.
Our bodies do the harvesting.
Grains and nuts.
Beans, fruits and vegetables.
We will grow enough to feed the world.

Kelli Arakaki-Bond

ARTEMIS UNDERGOES A SEX CHANGE

Artemis
womb of the world
my namesake
they unsexed you.

Great Mother
who gave every mountain, every wheat field
every bear stag lion wolf child wild beast
birth
they chastened you.

Banished you to the woods
a virgin, a forever-boy
with troops of campfire girls
and bitches
to bait bear, stalk boar, and
hack the living heart and hoof
from an occasional man-beast
to glut your rage.
Transformer,
they transformed you.

They cut off your lactating breasts
drained the Mediterranean of your warm milk
usurped your menstrual moon throne
and handed back a bloodless stone,
an Easter seal
to roll across your womb
and only then allowed themselves

to worship
what was left of you.
But they aren't going to do
any of that to me.

Artemis
womb of my words
transformer
I'll transform you.

Diana Azar

HERA GETS WHAT SHE DESERVES

In high school she vice-presidented
every organized virtue,
got to make rules
because she broke none,
led cheers, flag waving from the sidelines,
kicked only to show off
her Alpha Beta Leggs.

Betty Crocker of the ancient world
she switched her Mount Olympus major to Home Ec,
transformed volcano-tossed salads
into strict molds of jello,
bartered her goodhousekeeping
sealed Safeway hymen for a diamond ring.
A good girl masquerading as prom queen
she got what she deserved—
a bad boy disguised as a king.

Goddess of the joke, marriage and sacred cows
of all that binds, limits and weighs,
laws contract lifetime recipes,
she cooked her nuptial goose behind
bars on a gilded cage. Zeus was her fowl,
the one she wouldn't let Time eat,
the one she never wanted to let out.
Disguised as a pathetic shivering bird
he quivered on her warming breast,
worming his way into her
green apple pie heart.
But when the worm became a snake
her thighs, wedlocked, slammed shut.

Great Lady still in residence
in the ancient temple of all female hearts,
you should have canceled your lifetime
subscription to Greek family weekly
shooed Schlafly pie pandowdy from the palace
left the ladies' home on the heart
taken lovers (sometimes two wrongs make a right)
divorced the dauphin so he could become a king
as wives have to divorce themselves from you
before you can become
Great Queen of the Sacred Marriage
between Earth and Heaven
you are but so far never been.

Diana Azar

AMAZON

Her right breast—
the one the Amazons lopped off
the better to draw the bow—
dominant twin, the blossom
her lovers preferred
to inhale and to taste,
used to be lovelier than its mate
before the surgeon's knife
nipped off her American beauty rose
and grew an Amazon warrior where
a pretty pink blossom had been.

Diana Azar

HALF A MAN IS BETTER THAN ONE

My married lover comes and goes
I do not have to wash his clothes.
Into my house my lover steals
I do not have to cook his meals.
His money's theirs and mine is mine;
though he has more I am just fine.
In case of an emergency
I decide who what when, not he.
If I stay out till three a.m.
he does not ask me where I've been.
Our passion flares, our passion cools
I'm not the one my lover fools.
The only tie securing me
is pleasure in his company.
Coming together or apart
I am the secret of his heart.
Married women who pity me
don't understand: I'm free, I'm free.

Diana Azar

MORE BIZARRE THAN A ZEBRA

Slats of sunlight through Venetian blinds
make art
more bizarre than a zebra
more striking than a Mondrian
more perfectly formed than a fugue
more varied than tales
from A Thousand and One Nights.

Where is the artist?
I would like to thank her.

Diana Azar

MAJDANEK, APRIL 1973

It looks like any meadow. Sheep might safely
graze here, or lie oblivious to the April
drizzle. These buildings should be barns, or should
have been. But were. Terminology
will fail us: built for beasts, vacant now,
weathered to mellow brown they mutely stand
windowless, dark and blank. We wait in vain
to sense past horrors; even the barbed wire
coiled in the ditches glistens with raindrops
blinking rainbowed diamonds, the treasured dew
sweetening the tangled weeds. Pastoral thoughts
persist, until the future impinges on
the mind. Too quaint. Too picturesque, the place
is too available. Ready for use,
it stands. We would tear it down. But worse
to forget, some say. The residue of sin
colossal not original. There is
no remedy for past or future here:
only the thing itself. We can make
nothing of it, forever.

Helen Jaskoski

Florence, August 1987

*(Botticelli burned his paintings in Savonarola's bonfires
of vanities.)*

They are burning the fields of Tuscany.
Over the hills in the river sands beyond the pine
mountains smoke
ascends
the sky is brown
no one can breathe under this pall of acrid smoke
in Arezzo in Lucca
from the white mountains of Carrara to the swamps
of malarial
Maremma
they are burning burning
tomato vines squash vines
mullein and burdock
in the city of Savonarola as well and the final remains
of edible thistles: artichokes.
No one is home
cities and villages are shut down.
All have gone to the sea
bathing and riding on wind sails and in Viareggio a man
throws a small net carefully folded out from one arm it opens
like an umbrella and he comes dripping to shore with
shining tiny fish.
The Verazzano family, still selling their oils and wine
to the tourists
driving by: "OLIO, VINO, VENDITA DIRITTA" Direct Sales so
say the signs and one day
one of them will sail into New York harbor and be
remembered forever
in a bridge far from the cypresses and pines and vines
swelling full, the
bunches pendulous with promise.

In Florence a fire is burning Allessandro throws in
his paintings
we never know what they are or were or will be:
Venus and Cupid, delicacy
and fine bodies
into the fire of Savonarola's penance. In the city
such things are happening.
In the evening in the country, under the smoke-filled
sky, farmers
recline at table, men, women, children
they eat olives, bread and sheep's cheese
their faces lit in the blue glow of the television,
they take last year's red wine, and water
from the mineral springs where in winter
they will ease their bodies into the hot sulphur springs
and pack their limbs in mud also exported
to Florida.
They watch the newcomers, sandaled and jewelled
the strangers who will bring writing and chisels and
send away
cattle and wine, olives and grain
out in ships
and name the world
America the moons of Jupiter, the Sea of Tranquility.
The marble mountains move piece by piece
they open like eggs for the tombs of San Lorenzo
under the ground
in the cool of the earth live
the dead in their circular city
one entrance to north south east west
they eat and drink and make love
under the burning fields of Tuscany
under the brown August sky.

Helen Jaskoski

Last Will And Testament

i

Crouched inside myself

Under the hard shale
Of my skull,
Under the trees
Growing out of my armpits,
Behind the tangle
Sprouting out
Of my thighs

Watching the dust
drift down
Between my toes —
Dry auguries
of things to come.

Feeling my warped bones
Grind together
when I practice separations
to my Jane Fonda cassette,
and my joints,
those knobby fiddles
that no longer
vibrate to love,
hollow as drinking
straws as they sip up
death's sweet soda.

As I dissolve
slowly into swamp gas
and peat.

Let me leave
this last will
and testament
just in case
someone sees
these coronas
of blue light

ii

So now, let me start:
One if by land and two, by sea,
bravely:

I, Priscilla Oaks,
a resident of the city
of Laguna Beach, in the County
of Orange,
State of
California?

being of sound
and disposing mind
and memory,
and not acting
under fraud, duress, menace
or undue influence
of any person or persons,
do hereby make,
publish and declare
this to be
my Last Will and Testament.

First,

I leave all
my bra hooks
and an empty plywood
guitar case
covered with black
alligator-grained plastic
to my ex-husband.

he used to move his hands
under my sweater
in the back
to snap the elastic strap
twanging my breasts,
like jai-alai balls,
and grabbing them
as sex signals.

"I sure know how to tune you up,"
he'd say
"You're so lucky
to have me!"

Darling, I'm grateful!

To my son, I leave
a ton, a warehouse
full of 2 by 5 1/2 foot
cardboard sheets,
to cut into perfect
mothers, at least
a fifty year supply
to color, tear, burn,
attack, display
for show-and-tell
or throw away.

Nobody can say
I wasn't generous
and never gave
of myself.

and to my daughters,
all three
adorable babies
without any colic
or terrible childhood diseases
no trouble at all,
until they became
teen agers,

to them, I leave
a single copy of
FASCINATING WOMANHOOD

for fighting over,
a can of worms
to open up
and fish with
in whatever waters
they are muddying,
plus, most generous
and personal,
all my white stretch
marks from their pregnancies.

What else?
for my father, of course,
that incredible screamer
who terrified my childhood,
to him, I return his gifts:
my brains
that always come to conclusions
too lightning fast
and frighten men,

and my myopic eyes
that always see the truth
out of focus
until too late
to do anything.

as for my sister,
let me return
in brown wrapping paper,
the generous portion
of hissing paranoia
and insecurity
she lent me as a child.
Her house is full,
so she can store it
in her garage
in case she runs
out of supplies.

That's all for the family
right now
except for a few cousins
I haven't seen in years
and a niece
made of barracudas
who needs no bitterness
from me.

The masculine, feminine
or neuter genders,
shall each be deemed
to include the others.
I don't know
what that means
but it sounds warm
and friendly
like a party,

and you're supposed
to put it in.

Oh yes, and finally,
my friends and lovers!
They're not
forgotten
but will share
a separate will
of hope and joy.
I have intentionally
and with full knowledge
omitted them from this
foregoing instrument,
although they are welcome
to come to the party.

Priscilla Oaks

HAVE-A-HEART TRAPS

by Diana Azar

It's the tenth anniversary of the Fall of Saigon, and one of my housemates, probably Dan — Joshua has no stomach for real life — has left the TV on. All week I have been treated to fire-bombed villages before my morning coffee, so I head for the set to turn it off. As I pass the downstairs bathroom, a flow of obscenities leaks out from behind the closed door. I am unnerved by their coarseness, though I recognize my housemate Joshua's gentle voice. What he is doing, for at least the third time this week, I can't imagine, and I'm too polite to ask.

In the family room, helmeted newsreel cops sic snarling dogs into a throng of students protesting the Vietnam war. Dan has probably left for work, but just in case he hasn't, I turn off the sound. I can bear the hysteria of violence more easily with one of my senses shut down, but when a guardsman clubs a student's head, knocking him to his knees and opening a gash through which dark blood begins to ooze, I turn away and pop my croissant in the microwave.

As I reach for my decaf behind Dan's meat substitute and Joshua's tofu — I'm the only carnivore in my house — something hairy scampers out from under the fridge, brushing my ankles as it races by. I drop the coffee can, spraying the floor with fine, dark grounds. A scratchy sound at the window over the sink cuts off my expletives as I stoop to pick up the empty can. Outside on the window ledge, between my potted cactus and Joshua's fragile begonia, a plump neighborhood cat, back arched, claws at the screen. I stamp the floor, lunge forward and hiss "Scat!" But the fat El Dorado cats who've taken over my patio are unimpressed by steel-belted, marshmallow threats like mine. This one plops down on the ledge to await any opportunity to penetrate the flimsy barrier between her and the mouse.

I'm on my knees cleaning up the mess when Joshua quietly appears. A textbook ectomorph with narrow shoulders and a 5'8" body nature ironed out to 6'2", Joshua stands there inert, asking no questions, offering no help. He is monkish in his habits, shy, young enough to be my son, and we have lived together for three years, without so much as one cross word. I'm reconciled to his passivity. I scan him for some clue to his bizarre bathroom behavior before I say, "We have to do something about that goddamned mouse."

"What do you have in mind?"

"What do you think?" I slash my throat with my finger, wishing the mouse could disappear down the drain as easily as the coffee grounds it made me spill. "I hate to do him in after so many weeks of peaceful coexistence, but coffee's four dollars a pound."

Joshua nods. "He used to be discreet. But yesterday I found mouse droppings in my bran."

I look at the cat coiled on the ledge a scant two feet away. I prefer dogs to cats, though cats do not allow themselves to be trained to attack crowds. Though I cannot imagine this overfed gray one taxing herself to catch a mouse, I can imagine her seizing an unearned opportunity. I slide the window shut.

"There's a mousetrap in the garage," I tell Joshua. Though I respect few sex-specific divisions of labor, I decide this is one of them. "I'll get the trap. You get the mouse."

In the adjoining family room, a U.S. Army sergeant is stuffing three legs and an arm into a body bag. He hoists the bag onto a huge hook dangling from a chopper. Whirring blades churn up a typhoon in his hair. An invisible camera eye cuts to the student clutching the gash in his head. Between his fingers, the once oozing blood now pours. "Mind if I change the channel?" Joshua asks.

I dry my hands and walk out on the patio en route to the garage. The cat opens one eye, a narrow yellow slit, to admit me begrudgingly into consciousness. I wag a finger at her and declaim, "You're next!" She yawns, exposing her pink throat, then rearranges her tail on the ledge. I search the dark green, elephant-eared plant beds and spot two more neighborhood cats concealed among rubbery leaves. They are the only visitors that Joshua ever has. I pass from a shaft of white sunlight into the cool dark of the garage.

As the automatic garage door rises, two pairs of legs, a woman's and a man's, race past. Dan has remembered to take out the garbage. The newspapers he sets on top have disappeared; the lid of one plastic can is askew. Two doors down the alley, a shabbily dressed Mexican man and his wife are loading newspapers into a crumbling pick-up truck with tires worn down to the cords. They look at me with frightened faces. I smile to indicate I've no objection to their salvaging whatever they can from my garbage, but they do not smile back. The man keeps an eye on me as I stoop to retrieve the El Dorado Courier News. The woman, hands dangling from limp wrists, waits for his go-ahead to explore my neighbors' trash. I feel sorry for them and remember a bag of good used clothing I have set aside. I lug it out from its place near the shiny bicycles Dan, Joshua and I never use. It's heavy so I put it back. I arrange a smile on my face as I approach the truck. But the Mexicans misunderstand anyway, leap into the truck, and drive off in the opposite direction.

Inside the condo, Joshua's switching channels. All seem to carry the same thing. The Fall of Saigon ten years ago is bigger news than the Fall of Adam as hundreds, thousands of Vietnamese rush the Embassy gate, clawing their way up chain link fences and over barbed wire to drop into the Embassy compound below. Even the TV evangelists have interrupted their apocalyptic begging, more obsessed by their expulsion from Saigon than from Eden. Snakes, rats, toads everywhere. Everywhere gardens transformed into jungles. Everywhere except here in fashionable El Dorado where Joshua turns from images splitting the screen apart like gunfire in a Hollywood Western showdown, and says in a voice softer than a baby's skin, "I've changed my mind."

He gazes sorrowfully at the tiny wooden mousetrap in my hand.

"Come on, Joshua, give me a break! Those aren't mouse droppings in your bran, they're rat turds. Don't think of it as killing a defenseless field mouse. Think of it as saving the world from plague-carrying rats."

Joshua smiles shyly at the floor. "You do it then."

"Me?" I tap the mousetrap to my chest. It leaves a trail of dirt on my clean blouse. "You want me to do it?"

Joshua shrugs shoulders as narrow as his hips and clicks the television off. A boy with half his face missing disappears from the screen. The door chimes ring. Joshua looks up and says, "Saved by the bell."

Two women, one Asian, one white, stand on my porch. Though only in their thirties, they are dressed like matrons in unstylish clothes. The Asian stands behind the one in a seersucker dress with a Peter Pan collar who does all the talking. "Hi there," she says. "We're canvassin' your neighborhood this mornin' for the Lord and — "

"I'm not interested." My tone is clipped and firm.

"We'd like to leave a message with you just in case you change your mind."

I open the screen door to take the flyer in the hand that's not holding the mousetrap.

"Who was it?" Joshua asks.

"Salespeople."

Joshua reaches behind his meditation cushion for his thongs. "What did you decide to do? About the mouse?"

I glance down at the flyer: HAVE YOU GOT THE HOLY SPIRIT? and say, "Wait till Dan gets home."

Dan and I sit on the floor in front of the TV. I'm combing his hair out — it's thicker than a rat's nest — while four men and a woman discuss what went wrong in Vietnam. Dan spent some time in Canada after his draft board denied him status as a conscientious objector because he did not belong to a church. He didn't like Canada much — it was too cold — so he phoned his father, who thought war in Vietnam a grand idea, and told him he planned to be home in time for his twentieth birthday. Two FBI agents arrested him in front of his father's house the day he arrived. After a lawyer he still owes thousands of dollars to had him declared mentally incompetent, he won a scholarship to a small private college, majored in math and now works for an El Dorado high-tech corporation where he's bound to a low rung of the corporate ladder by a contempt for polyester, an FBI agent he suspects is still following him around, and an unruly mane on which I've already broken three combs.

"I don't know why you keep going on job interviews." I place my feet against Dan's back for leverage as I pull the hairbrush through his matted hair.

"Ouch!"

"Careful!" Dan has a glass of cranberry juice on a saucer on the floor. "Spill that on my beige carpet and I'll pluck out every hair on your head one by one."

"You say that every night and I haven't spilled one drop of anything yet."

I fist what I can of Dan's hair at the back of his neck, but most of it continues to resist. Three feet from the end of my nose, two U.S. soldiers question a bird-boned, shirtless Vietnamese boy they have flushed from a field. The combat boot of one pins the captive's shoulder to the ground while the other soldier jabs a bayonet into his throat. "Aren't you ready for Eye on L.A.?" I ask.

The cranberry juice has stained Dan's lips red. "I want to see what I missed. It helps me sustain the delusion that fucking up my life somehow improved the world."

I take a fistful of Dan's hair, clutch it, and pull the brush through the entangled vine below. "No company will ever hire you or promote you until you get rid of some of this. That's the best I can do. Don't be surprised if guys start whistling at you from behind."

"Anything's better than a Nazi-Fascist haircut from Linear Inc." Dan picks up the hand mirror on the floor to examine my work and adds, "Almost."

The rubber band in Dan's pony tail snaps. His hair explodes just as a bomb bursts through a roof marked with a cross in Ho Chi Minh City. The mouse runs out from behind the TV. My breath plunges into reverse as I make a grab for Dan's arm. Dan knocks over the cranberry juice. I leap up, rush into the adjoining kitchen for a sponge to stop the spread of the dark stain. Dan's sopping up what he can with the hem of his shirt and stammering apologies. "I'll forgive you," I say, as Dan wipes off his simulated leather shoes. He shuns real leather for the same reasons he shuns real meat: he's against killing sentient beings for human convenience or pleasure. "On one condition."

"I get the carpet cleaned?"

"You kill the mouse. Joshua can't bring himself to do it and neither can I."

"There's no need for any of us to do it. We'll catch the mouse without hurting it and then let it go."

I wring the dark red juice out of the sponge and say, "Yeah? How?" Behind Dan's back a corporal nudges bodies with his rifle butt and the toe of his combat boot — leather, no doubt — into an overcrowded grave. "For Christsake, can't you turn that damn thing off?"

"No," Dan replies. "I wish I could."

I have spent the morning driving to four El Dorado hardware stores in search of a means to protect me and my housemates from a mouse that will protect the mouse from us as well. The clerk at the store I phoned first told me that they had such a device, but when I appeared another clerk told me the store no longer carried it; it didn't sell. Next to a sign: ERADICATE RODENTS, DEAD RATS DON'T COME BACK, he held up the usual wooden trap whose spring can break a mouse in half and said, "What's wrong with the old-fashioned way? It's easy, inexpensive, and it works."

"Not for the mouse," I said and feeling noble, left.

The HAVE-A-HEART trap in the brown paper bag on the seat beside me now is larger and cost more than the tiny trap whose spring can break a mouse in half. I divide by three and tell myself it's a lifetime investment as I pull into the alley behind my house. It isn't garbage day, but community association workers from TANAKA — GARDENS OF EDEN are trimming my tract's trees. The air rings with buzz-saws, heavy equipment trucks and chains. Small piles of wood and severed tree limbs dot the curbsides, awaiting pick up. The crumbling truck is parked under the trees; its faded-to-no-color hood sprouts cast-off purple blossoms from the jacaranda trees above. The Mexican man and his wife are nowhere in sight.

I aim my garage door opener and pull in before the door's all the way up. I get out of my car and peer round my open garage door to see if anyone's in the alley. No one is. I lug the bag of good used clothing, washed, ironed and ready to wear, from its place by the near-new bikes Dan, Joshua and I gave ourselves last Christmas with the intention of keeping in shape with rides to man-made De Oro Lake but which, somehow, we never use. I trudge down the alley toward the crumbling pick-up as fast as I can, given the weight I carry. As I heft the bag of clothes onto a fender, a hot, dry Santa Ana wind blows my hair in my face. My inner eye cuts to a soldier wrestling with a body bag as I shove my bag over the guard rail into the truck. The Mexican leaps up from the truckbed. My hand flies to my heart as I reel back, suck in my breath. Up close, he looks unsavory. His face is puffy from the snooze I've interrupted. His dark, leathery head bows once, twice, when he sees me. Though we seem fated to misunderstand each other, I do what I can in my high school Spanish to explain what I am up to.

"*Si, si, 'sta bien,*" he says, quick to absolve me of all blame. His gestures suggest that the very notion I could be to blame for anything, ever, is as preposterous as the notion he could be blame-free, especially in fashionable El Dorado. His wife appears, lugging some wood; she looks exhausted, much older than she probably is. Her teeth — the ones not missing — are brown with decay. She smiles when her husband points to the plastic bag, but her smile fades when I say no, the bag contains no toys or children's clothes. "*Pa'la Navidad,*" she says, though Christmas is six weeks away. How many children does she have, I ask. Thirteen. I nod and say one must plan for Christmas ahead.

Dan's home from work because when I enter my condo through the rear patio door, a GI, cradling his dead buddy in his arms, sobs in my family room, and no one's watching. The HAVE-A-HEART trap I set on the breakfast counter is a metal house, the size of a small TV. The bait goes in the house, the mouse goes after it; as in marriage, crossing the threshold makes the door slam shut, trapping the mouse. I cut a chunk of extra sharp cheddar and slip it deep into the house. I set the house on the floor by the fridge where the mouse goes to slake his thirst, then head toward the downstairs bathroom. I'm drawn up short by the obscenities flowing through the closed door. Before I can retreat, the door opens. Joshua and I nearly collide.

"Sorry." I back up at once.

No dark circles under Joshua's eyes. No telltale flush of pink upon his creamy cheeks. His skin's as soft and smooth as a baby's bottom although Joshua is twenty-three years old. "I guess you're wondering what I'm doing in there," he says with a shy smile.

"Well, yes, to tell the truth, I am."

Joshua follows me into the family room where a rocket explodes on a busy Saigon street. Everyone starts to run. Cut to a close up of a face with no expression. Cut to another, looking back as everyone begins to run. No one stops to assist those on fire who fall. The voiceover says the Vietnamese are used to this. I wonder how one gets used to being on fire, but I wonder more what Joshua has been up to in the bathroom. I turn off the sound and say "Ahh, peace."

Joshua is too shy to meet my gaze but manages to say, "My therapist suggested I get in touch with my anger."

I do not reply at once. Then I say, "Who are you angry at? Not me, I hope."

"I'm not angry at anyone. My therapist suggested that saying bad words might put me in touch with my aggressive feelings." Joshua blushes. "He says I'm too good. I don't have any fun."

"A volleyball class would accomplish the same thing and it's much cheaper than a therapist. You might meet someone your own age, make friends, completely change your life."

Joshua tunes in to a different channel, a children's program, and says, "Yes, I know."

That night, while a French nun in a Vietnamese orphanage feeds a child with no arms, I tell Joshua and Dan about the Mexican couple, their thirteen children and the bag of adult clothes with no toys. Joshua, who needs half an hour to decide between an apple or a pear for lunch, would like to sleep on my suggestion that we give away the bikes we never use. Dan contends that the bikes, especially his and Joshua's, are too big for children. I counter that a family with thirteen children is bound to have some that the bikes will fit. Dan says no creature big enough to ride his bike could possibly be classified a "child." He faults my common sense and charges me with confusing compassion and sentimentality. Joshua points out the family could sell the bikes and use the money to buy presents for the younger children. Dan says he should do that himself and apply the money to legal debts dating back to his refusal to kill any beings he won't eat. Joshua expresses surprise that Dan still owes court costs and legal fees after so many years. Dan reminds Joshua that, unlike Joshua, he is not a banker's son. Joshua asks Dan what that's supposed to mean. Thinking how pleasant it would be to ride across town to De Oro Lake and feed the ducks, I say I'm sorry I brought up the bikes; why don't we all just let it drop.

Next morning when I come downstairs, Dan's on his way out the front door. He tells me I can have his goddamned bike and shuts the door before I can reply. Joshua's in the bathroom getting in touch with his aggression, while two Viet Cong youths proudly display the severed ears and nose of a South Vietnamese regular. I turn away in haste to see if HAVE-A-HEART traps work.

I cock an ear against the metal house and hear the mouse scratching around inside. I lift the trap slowly — I do not want to traumatize the mouse — and carry it outside. I check the ledge — no cat — before I kneel down by the Henri Rousseau jungle-dark plant beds that frame my patio's edge. Through the open back door of the garage, I notice the main garage door is wide open onto the alley. I must have forgotten to close it the day before after I hauled away the bag of clothes. Cut to a large bare space big enough for three bicycles as my hand slides open the HAVE-A-HEART trap door. Cut to a tiny mouse leaping out, a cat pouncing from behind a jungle of elephant-eared plants. The cat dives back into the foliage as Joshua slides open the glass patio door.

"I've decided to let them have my bike."

"I'm very glad to hear it." I smile through an apocalyptic dread for all of us — him, Dan, myself, the Mexican man and his wife. Joshua's nod is serene, possibly beatific. "Maybe you ought to find another therapist."

Joshua steps back into the house. I can't turn off the sound of thrashing in the dark plant bed beside me. Through the glass patio door, I see an Asian girl of seven or eight, mouth open in a scream I cannot hear, running toward me from my family room. She is naked and on fire.

RECEIVING KRISTA LUANA, THE KAHUNA

by Kelli Arakaki-Bond

For Lorree, bringing food up means bringing her down. Like at the age of seven, when it was an entire enchilada lunch, a rolling out of the red carpet for the janitors at her grammar school. The culprit: a mocha-colored pill normally given to children who are mentally retarded and prone to marathon weeping.

But Lorree was neither feeble-minded nor constantly teary. A psychiatrist had prescribed the mood elevators upon the insistence of Lorree's own mama. Mama, between filling an ashtray with one pack of Pall Malls in a single 50-minute session, recounted Lorree's at-home retreats with twelve imaginary characters. These, according to Mama, caused Lorree to incant phrases such as "brain-infected/disinfected," and to initiate games with the neighborhood children such as "The San Francisco Earthquake of 1906" and "The Great Chicago Fire." Lorree also loved prophesying hell and damnation to peers who misbehaved at school or at home, Mama said. Marginal behavior in a boy, but repulsive in a girl, she added.

Although the shrink said that Mama was practically de-stroying the makings of a future Pulitzer Prize novelist in Lorree, he capitulated to Mama's demands. Such dramatic evidence of Mama's fundamental intolerance towards Lorree as a person instilled a resolve in Lorree to, among other things, shun mind-altering substances in later life. This excluded aspirin six times a year, eight glasses of wine a year, or twelve allergy pills a year. Tonight, for the first time since the after-lunch episode in grade school 22 years ago, Lorree felt queasy.

"Couldn't be the allergy medication I took. Maybe it's what I ate this afternoon." Solaced by these thoughts, she went to bed.

The second hand on her clock on the nightstand swept a full circle when Lorree's stomach re-churned, fiercer and fiercer.

She lay on her right side. Then she placed her hands in front of her, palms down, and gently lowering them while chanting "down, down." No change. Repeating this ritual four different times in fifteen minutes made no dent.

As Lorree prepared to leap from the sheets for the bathroom, a woman stood at the bedroom door wearing an icy pink silk holoku which formed wings when she stretched her arms to her sides. Orchid, ferns, white and lavender statice, yellow cushion mums and a ti leaf on raffia — haku lei — caressed the women's bun of white hair. A setting of diamonds and opal rested on the woman's throat.

Lorree gasped. She felt as though she had met this woman before, perhaps as one of the dozen make-believe people she chatted with in the old days.

"Oh, my God," Lorree whispered as she became entranced by this six-foot column of femininity now looming over Lorree's bed. Even in her nausea, Lorree reached out to stroke the rose quartz-colored gown that ordinarily draped a bride and female guest of honor in the Hawaiian culture.

"My name is Krista Luana," the woman intoned in a deep, guttural voice. "Go ahead. Please touch." Krista Luana's aquamarine eyes, uplifted at the corners, reinforced the invitation.

As Lorree fingered the diamonded studded edges of Krista Luana's sleeves, Krista Luana said, "Give up your silly mantra. 'Down, down.' What's that supposed to mean? I'm here. I'm your goddess — your kahuna — to help you get over your sickness."

Lorree recoiled. "Krista Luana — or... is... it... really Christopher Louis? Get... out! Kahunas... are... men!"

"Not necessarily..." Krista Luana trailed off when Lorree cut in, "You're a mahu, in drag no less. What's more, kahunas cast bad spells. Hexes!"

"Calm down," Krista Luana reassured. "I'm a woman, all flesh and bone. At birth! Not an ounce of silicone or foam padding on me. Never wished for anything different below the waist. But that's beside the point. Kahunas can be priestesses or medicine women, bring good luck."

Lorree's jaws dropped. "But... but... but...," she stammered, "you're... so... beautiful that it's almost too good to be real. You can pass for one of the girls at Finocchio's, that theatre with men who dress like women in San Francisco. I feel like scum next to you. I feel like I should go brush my hair, or at least gargle with Listerine."

"Nonsense," Krista Luana countered. "I love you just as you are. Now, why don't you lie down, or else you'll be retching worse than you ever have."

Krista Luana arranged an arc of white votives atop mint sprigs on Lorree's night table. She lifted Lorree's nightgown. She worked her fingers above Lorree's hip bones, into the appendix area, even into the beginnings of "love handles."

When Krista Luana found the spot right above Lorree's navel, she placed a tiny yellow diamond there and whispered, "I want you to close your eyes and follow my voice." Lorree moaned softly as Krista Luana continued massaging.

"In the days not so long ago," she started, "there lived some women. For them, the idea of fast food was absurd. That kind of garbage would have stopped them from working the land where they cultivated anise and peppermint. When these herbs were ready, they were ground into powder. Each was steeped in kettles of water. No need for the goop you find in Seven-Up or ginger ale. I know that's what you'd like to drink because everyone's always told you that calms an upset stomach."

Lorree eeked out, "That's true... "

Krista Luana asked, "Well, then, would you to try something like these crones made?"

"I... I... don't know." Lorree was frightened of losing her grip on her surroundings and people, the hold she outwardly perfected 21 years back to fend off further doses of anti-depressants.

"Oh, be brave!" Krista Luana insisted. "You'll be secure in this room. I'll be right here."

"But what if I never return? How are you going to rescue me then?"

"Believe me, you'll come back. You'll be tethered to my

voice at all times, so there's no way of getting lost."

"All right."

"Now, I'm going to draw a white circle of light around you. Relax and breathe deeply through your nose." Lorree seemed to recede into the mattress.

"Inhale. Exhale," Krista Luana instructed. "That's right. Breathe deeply. Inhale. Exhale. Now let yourself float down a spiral staircase. Move inward and down."

Eyelids fluttering, Lorree murmured in response to Krista Luana's guidance. From this, Krista Luana surmised that Lorree was now in a trance.

"You've now reached the bottom of this staircase. Look around you. You're now in the vestibule next to the kitchen of these women. The women want you to go to the cutting board. On that board lies three separate bundles of greens. Examine them carefully. Pick them up. Sniff them. Hold them. Take time to pick the one that's right for you."

After remaining silent for a couple of minutes, Krista Luana asked Lorree, "What herb did you choose?"

"Chamomile."

"Good," Krista Luana said as she continued stroking Lorree's solar plexus. Now see yourself fixing the chamomile. Let me know when you're done." Krista Luana quieted for another five minutes before Lorree gave her the high sign.

"The women kegged mixtures like anise, peppermint, and chamomile to use when one had nausea," Krista Luana said. Lorree sunk deeper and deeper, enfolding Krista Luana's suggestions.

"See before you a silver cup," Krista Luana said. "It's sterling. Polished. Just for you. Take this cup and set it under the spigot for chamomile. Fill your cup. Take your time to watch that soothing liquid cascade into that cup."

Although she appeared asleep, Lorree parted her lips as if to sip the tea.

"Let the chamomile course over your tongue," Krista Luana prodded. "Let it pour down your throat. As it reaches your stomach, you find a pair of lock floodgates. They're weighing you down. Let the chamomile push these gates open.

Now watch these gates, that bad blood, fall off their hinges and move downstream with the flow of the chamomile. You've just flushed yourself of all gastric pain."

Before Krista Luana could finish, Lorree was snoring. Krista Luana traced stars, moons and hearts under Lorree's diaphragm, then lowered Lorree's nightgown back over her calves. Covering Lorree with a lavender afghan, Krista Luana kissed her forehead and blew out the candles.

Victim Of Nice

by Sarie Sachie Hylkema

I enter the house after a frustrating and stressful day at work. Chester greets me with a leap against my knee. I say my usual welcome and admonish him for jumping on my good suit.. The floor is covered with Kapok stuffing he has dug out of his sleeping cushion. I am not ready to deal with much more; I am happy to be home; Chester at least missed me.

As I step into the living room, I see that my former husband is paying our son Eric a visit in his bedroom. I feel a seriousness about them in the way they are conversing. I put my hand out as if to feel the water; it feels hot and somehow foreboding. And putting aside the weight of my day at work, I stepped in.

The father of my son tells me he spent the weekend at a seminar with the Man Woman Institute. From the seminar, he learned that women are angry and therefore "mean" to the men in their lives. "Women's anger does not allow men to win in the game of relationship," he said. He does point out that it is justifiable for women to be angry considering their invalidation and their treatment. Then he looked at me eye to eye, and only a few inches from my face and said, "You're mean."

The anger in me burned my bowels like hot stones.

Even in my rage, I knew I needed to speak without anger to be clearly heard. With my voice slightly elevated and a tremble that I squeezed to keep my emotions tightly contained, I said, "You're damn right women are angry and doubly so with Asian women! Asian American women especially have had to hide their anger with sweetness and niceness."

I felt like an overblown balloon that had exploded and with the release of the air, I was bathed with a sense of curiosity, a moment of clarity. Although my ex-husband and I have been separated and divorced for fifteen years, I wondered why his words still evoked the cry that hid inside. I asked myself, "did I still care?" That was not the issue in this case. He only represents a whole class of people; voices of authority that we have been traditionally taught to learn and obey. And my angry outburst reminded me that I wanted to be independent and free of the emotional baggage that continues to rear its head.

We women have been victims of nice because being victims and being nice were expected of us. These roles are especially inherent in Asian women who have spent their entire lives trying to please their men: their grandfathers, their fathers and their husbands. But we don't feel nice; nice has been imposed on us. And we are nice people. The other side of the coin is someone like me, who has felt the anger, intuitively acknowledged the anger and tried to either remedy or deal with it on an intimate level. I did not feel nice going through the process.

As a child, I sensed my mother's frustration over her powerlessness. I felt the overpowering, immovable cultural restrictions that frustrated her. She was a woman ahead of her time, especially for one who grew up in a little village on the island of Maui. She had seen life as an opportunity and had had her dreams. She was tough on us because she had it tough herself. She wanted us to have everything that was not available to her, and she watched in disappointment as it became clear to her that she could not remedy the situation even with her children. Only through time would the rigid grip of the culture be released. She sang when she did not want to remember her fate and hid her tears behind her song.

My mother is the model Japanese woman—hard working, courteous, gregarious, bright, pretty, tolerant, and an active member of her church. She is a good mother and daughter-in-law who always goes out of her way for others. I always wondered if anyone else knew that she was angry inside.

I am the eldest child and had responsibilities placed on me to look after my younger brothers and sisters. The family did not know how much of a responsibility that was for a small child, and I frequently felt heavy and scared inside. I did not know it then but I felt like a bad daughter when I did not meet the expectations of being the eldest and guilty when I wanted to be a child myself. Unconsciously, I was angry. I have always wondered why I was so intuitively sensitive to my mother and my grandmother. It is because I wore their shoes from an early age and became their silent partners.

I spent years trying to fix the anger; not only for me, but for my family and for what I thought was the Japanese culture. It was a hard lesson to realize that I could not fix it. The only way that I can rise out of my dilemma is to be aware of my anger. Together with all Asian American women, we need to confront our anger and release ourselves from this victimization.

Women have never had permission to be angry, let alone to show any signs of anger. We are afraid of showing anger because we would be condemned as bitchy or castrating. We are afraid of being in touch with our anger. What would we do with it if we were? And so the quiet seething continues.

I thought I had the advantage over many women, especially Asian American women. I was not going to pretend that I was everything that a Japanese woman should be and I communicated this to others around me, often in frustration. My position felt scary at times and unpopular. It was difficult because a large part of me wanted everyone to like me and I sometimes felt very alone. To an extent, I have been fortunate as I have been able to have my own identity instead of trying to maintain the image of some prescribed Japanese American woman.

The disadvantage is that I never felt grounded, never sure that I was doing the right thing for me. I made some Japanese women uncomfortable because I intruded into their pretense. The majority of my family have supported me, even if they did not understand my actions or my feelings. They sometimes wished that I would be less harsh on myself and accept things the way they were.

I have always wished that I could be a little softer or feel that I am softer. I didn't always want to appear to be strong and forward; sometimes I wanted to be sweet like a nice Japanese woman. And yet I thought I would be giving up something if I always acted sweet and coy. It always seemed manipulative to sweetly ask for something, even though I saw that it worked for most women. Why can't I be independent, straight speaking, and feminine as well? Again, this imposed standard of how a Japanese woman should be reverts to the cause her anger.

Some men are intimidated by my words, at least men who have been in relationship with me. And these relationships have not turned out the way I had hoped. It could very well be that my anger colored the way I presented myself to them. Of course, men have played a large part in holding us in our anger by confirming the lack of our femininity whenever we use strong words or act out our anger. According to them anger is unattractive in a woman. We think that suppression of anger makes us attractive to men, but it ultimately causes the death of many relationships.

I also need to forgive the men in my life who have fueled my anger, without accepting their conspiracy, intentional or not. They have, after all, regarded women as second class citizens for eons. Men have a tremendous task ahead of them. They need to let go of their insecurity as human beings so that they may become equal partners with women. I will support them in their discovery and our partnership; I will not let them off the hook.

Letting go of my anger will free me of my resentment, but a healthy partnership will only work if men do likewise. Men have always been a large part of my life, starting with my father. My father held his anger inside too; I wanted to heal his silent pain since I was a little girl. As an adult, I always chose men who held their anger inside. I now look forward to having relationships with men who, like me, are no longer controlled by their anger.

Do I want to live my life as a Victim of Nice? I could continue to live as a victim of patriarchal and cultural injustices; or I could put all that garbage into a box and throw it away. The first step is to admit to my anger. Having done that, I need to choose. Part of the difficulty is finding a balance, a compromise in which I do not give up who I am and still be able to work out my anger. We need to not let our anger run our lives, but use it to propel us toward our potential.

Personally, I sometimes find myself confused by this

process of discarding the cultural baggage that is damaging to us. It is not an easy road as I see-saw in my ambivalence. There is the Japanese Sarie who still wants to be nice and to serve others. And there is the Japanese American Sarie who has learned that she can be expressive, independent, responsible, and committed to her own dreams without feeling like a bad person. It is this ambivalence that frustrates and angers me.

As women and men let go of these limiting legacies from generations before, we will become free to discover who we are. For too long we have been Victims of Nice.

THE CULT OF THE "PERFECT" LANGUAGE CENSORSHIP BY CLASS GENDER AND RACE.

by Mitsuye Yamada

Thanks to prodigious research by women scholars in the past two decades, we are beginning to see a fuller picture of women's history through recovered writings by them, that part of women's lives that has been left out of traditional literature and recorded documents. As the results of their research began to reach the popular market in the early 1970's, I read, with a sense of exhilarating excitement, the letters, diaries, poems, and songs collected in works such as *By a Woman Writt; Literature from Six Centuries by and About Women* and *The World Split Open; Four Centuries of Women Poets in English and America, 1552-1950.*[1] I was especially struck by what these women dared to "complain" about in their writings. The writers were not high-born ladies writing letters and poems to while away their time, but many were working women, either trying to make a living as popular writers or working in textile mills and mines. Such collections of recovered works give women, as one of the editors so aptly states, "their own voice in their own time." Among these diggings, I looked in vain for small nuggets, maybe a few specks, by my own immediate "mothers" in this country. Even in the more recent voluminous and extraordinary collection, *The Norton Anthology of Literature by Women*[2] a work that makes us acutely aware of "women's cultural situation" in a female context, early Asian women's voices are absent.

This article is an expanded version of a talk given at a Plenary Session at "Parallels and Intersections: A Conference on Racism and Other Forms of Oppression," sponsored and organized by Women Against Racism Committee, Women's Resource & Action Center, Univeristy of Iowa on April 8, 1989.

In the light of increasing interest in the experience of Asians in America, a similar search is under way among Asian American scholars to recover our historical past in this country. A few early polemical works in English have surfaced about the exclusion movement directed against the Chinese and Japanese immigrants in the late 19th C. and early 20th C., but generally research in this area has resulted in historical and sociological assessments by recent scholars about what happened *to* Asian immigrants. Very little has been written *by* the Asians themselves about how they were personally affected by nativist attitudes translated into anti-Asian immigration policies, except perhaps for those remarkable and poignant poems literally dug into the walls of the immigrant detention halls on Angel Island. The value of these has only been recently recognized, and the poems have been translated and published.[3] Finally, only in the past decade or so, have we begun to listen to the words of the old immigrants themselves as they reminisce about their early experiences in their native languages. A few oral history projects are under way to compile and translate these stories into English from their original languages. I have heard of a few personal diaries by first generation Issei[4] women, but they remain in the hands of their families, untranslated, and therefore inaccessible even to the diarists' own Nisei children. An exciting prospect for some future researcher in Asian Pacific American history may be to look for "letters home" which surely must exist among personal papers hidden away by families in boxes throughout Asia.

We now know that such writings, especially the intensely personal accounts, are building blocks to the dreams of future generations of writers. Had the writings by early immigrant Asian women been accessible in whatever form, they might have become grist for my own creative efforts when I was growing up. For myself, I yearn to read personal accounts by those Asian women who struggled beside their men. As I dipped into the above collections of women's writings, I felt a gnawing sense of regret that such primary materials by pioneering Asian women written "in their own voice in their own time" are almost nonexistent.

Meanwhile, what about the treasures that are being lost today as thousands of new Asian immigrants struggle to live, study, and work among us? We accept the loss as inevitable. Like those other Asians before them, we reason, they have no time for they are too busy working, studying, and becoming "acculturated." But all immigrants from different parts of the world have been faced with the same problems. In the early 1900's a number of Jewish and Italian immigrant writers, most notable among them Anzia Yezierska (*Bread Givers*, 1925), wrote about the day to day struggle of the immigrant in the New World. Among the Asians, we do have a few autobiographical works, but on the whole, except for Carlos Bulosan's writings, they are "East meets West" observations designed to charm the hearts of American readers. Could there be other factors involved that make Asians, more than other immigrants, reluctant to openly express themselves? Can they be persuaded to tell us in any language they now speak, in any way they know, something about the function of culture and myth that shapes our lives? If our past history is any guide, probably not, except for those who are writing for the many foreign language weekly newspapers in their own communities. As for the rest of the immigrants, they are caught in "the cult of the 'perfect' language." Their lives are in constant transition as are their languages, but a crucial part of their life experiences may never be recorded.

Through examining my own culture, my mother's experiences as an immigrant woman and my own experience as a Japanese American, I will explore some of the cultural barriers that are peculiar with transplanted Asians, particularly the women. I belong to a still relatively small group called the Asian Pacific American Women Writers: the second, third, and fourth generation writers primarily educated in the American public school system. Very little in the literature, by men or women, that was given us during our school years spoke to our specific experiences. If we are now writing about our respective heritages from a vast array of Asian traditions, or about our identities within the American cultural landscape, or about our self-image in the American political context, we do so by forging our own way. A recently published anthology *The Forbidden Stitch,; An Asian American Women's Anthology*,[5] offers a nearly comprehensive bibliography but cites only a few works dated before 1970. Our Asian ancestors have been around for more than 150 years, but most of their experiences have never been recorded *in process* even in their own languages.[6]

Most of our writings are what we might call "retroflexive," bending back over territory trod by our parents or ourselves in a process of rebirth. Some of us, not aware at first of our "difference," had begun to write just as we began to perceive ourselves as "other" in a majority culture not our own, and of course by then we were writing in literate English. Even those of us who initially spoke another language didn't come out as writers until we became socially acceptable in English. Our main goal was to learn to write grammatical English and then to speak it without a trace of a foreign accent, if possible. Anything less, we assumed, would have been unacceptable. My ninety-year-old mother, for example, took English lessons seventy years ago for a short period and today speaks it only well enough to carry on a simple conversation with her grandchildren and great grandchildren. She gave up trying to learn years ago because, she says, she could "never, never get it right."

After my father's death more than thirty years ago, my mother came to live with my husband and me and our growing family of small children in suburban New York and moved with us to California several years later. In both places she felt isolated from old friends and from other Issei, the Japanese communities where my father and she usually lived before World War II in Seattle and in Chicago where they settled after that war. Helping us raise our children and watching the family dynamics among us had obviously triggered long-suppressed and anguished memories of "those early days" when she came to live with a man she hardly knew five-thousand miles away from family and friends in Japan. It was then that I began to hear touching stories I had never heard before: stories about her fears as a lonely young mother with small children, trying to cope in a strange country, separated from her immediate neighbors by language and culture. As the self-appointed family historian, I first started to record those stories by translating them into English, "for the sake of your Sansei grandchildren" I told her, but she would always admonish, "Don't write these things down; they aren't worth anything. It's too embarrassing; I hardly learned to speak English properly after all these years." She persisted in discrediting the value of her own stories because they could not be written down in proper style. I thought about capturing what she herself referred to as her special brand of "broken English." (The metaphor reflects our attitude toward those who do not speak as we do, as if language were an immutable artifact, like a precious marble statue, rather than a dynamic living force.)

The process seemed to me simple enough at first. All I had to do, I thought, was let her see her own words in print between the covers of a published book, and she would come to know that her language, and hence her experience, had a valid place in this culture. I wrote the poem "Marriage was a Foreign Country" and showed her the typed up version. (When we land the boat full/of new brides/lean over railing/with wrinkled glossy pictures/they hold inside hand/like this/so excited).[7] See Mother, here it is, these are your words, your life. But she would insist that I translate her words into "correct" English. When I countered that people would be more interested in hearing her real voice, she fretted that I was trying to expose her ignorance. She was adamant about my not embarrassing her by making her sound "crude and uneducated." I have tried to respect her wishes by "cleaning up" some of her most glaring grammatical errors and malapropisms, but because the emotional impact of her devastating experiences needed to be retained, I asked her if she would permit me to retain the flavor of her speech pattern in some way in the poem. She responded, "Sōshitara, warawarenai yōni shite chōdai;" then, don't make me into a laughing stock. Nobody will laugh at you, I would persist, but our conversations often ended with a variation of, "Yes they would because I sound like an illiterate lower-class person."

My mother is not the only person who associates language with class. Most Americans share the dictum that correct

English is spoken by proper well-educated Americans who use it to discuss serious matters; flawed English spoken with an accent (with the exception of the upper-class British accent) is spoken by the lower class and is usually the object of ridicule. The hierarchical language that existed in Japan when she was growing up, she found, was very much in force here as well.

My mother came to the United States at 19 years of age in 1918 to join my father who had earlier gone to Japan to "find a wife" and returned to his job in Seattle. She was born and raised in Fukuoka Prefecture on the island of Kyushu and speaks two different Japanese dialects: the Tokyo dialect considered to be the standard speech, and the country dialect of her prefecture. She had very carefully cultivated her Tokyo dialect to teach it to my three brothers and me. It was the dialect she used exclusively when she spoke in the company of her new friends among the immigrant Japanese in Seattle. I suggested to her that she write down those stories about her early days of adjustment to American culture in Tokyo dialect, exactly as she told them to me, but was puzzled when she even resisted that. Gradually, I learned what the problem was: through the years she learned that to the contemporary Japanese in her native land, her Tokyo speech, like that of most Issei here, had become old-fashioned and quaint after several decades of isolation from a changing mother tongue. Increasingly she became reluctant to even think of writing a letter to her educated relatives in Japan, she said, for fear of being judged unschooled by them.

I was undaunted. Well then, I said, why not write her stories down in her own country dialect, somewhat modified so that I could understand it. I remembered that she spoke another language besides the Tokyo dialect I knew. I learned this for the first time on our visit to Japan when I was a child. On that occasion, much to my astonishment, the minute we got off the train in Fukuoka, she began rattling off in a strange tongue to the throng of relatives who had come to meet us. This must have been her language, the language of her thoughts, but which she never permitted herself to reveal in full bloom even to us, her children. When I brought up this possibility she said, oh no, people would laugh. Didn't I know that country dialect, like street and peasant patois in print and on the stage, is often the language of light comedy in Japan (except, of course, to the native speakers). I had no quick response to this. I was reminded of the hillbilly speech which is often the subject of ridicule and scorn here. She brought up other examples: the *kyogen*, those short farcical and stupid antics of the commoners between performances of deadly serious Noh dramas. Ah yes, I would note, just like the comic relief segments in Shakespearean tragedies. I was amazed by the logic of her arguments but was nevertheless increasingly irritated by what I thought was her stubbornness.

In some ways, I was trying to find another project for my widowed mother who had become completely involved in her role as a mother substitute to my children since moving in with us. I tried different approaches. It's different in this country, I would tell her. People in America are charmed by country and other kinds of dialects because they are considered to be part of the folk culture like the patchwork quilts that she was so skillful at making. In fact, there are many written materials in the language of the Black people as well as in pidgin English spoken in Hawaii, I would say. But she could not be persuaded. She knew that these were not languages used for educated discourse or in serious writing.

At one point when she became tearfully defensive, I had to admit I was pressing too hard and finally realized she was not simply making excuses for herself. Here is a woman with incredible stories to tell who is capable of speaking and writing in three different languages but whose stories will never be recorded in any of those voices, because she herself has judged them flawed in some way. Separate social attitudes towards each of them, one reinforcing the other, have silenced her. In this country she faced the most common social attitudes towards her "broken English" almost on a daily basis. She remembers only too vividly the number of times salespersons shouted at her or spoke to her in a truncated childlike way as if she were hard of hearing or a person with limited mental faculties. *Hakujins* (white people), she complains, assume that people who speak less-than-perfect English or speak it with an accent (or both) are "flawed" in other ways. She became a victim of "the cult of the 'perfect' language" which exists even today in many other cultures as it does here. She is silenced multiply: by class attitudes towards language in both cultures, by herself in Japanese, and by us in English.

In addition to class attitudes that had the effect of self-censorship for my mother, strong gender-linked differences in Japanese speech must have compounded her difficulties in learning English as "perfectly" as she had hoped to. I had not realized until quite recently how much more complex learning a new language must have been for my mother than for some other immigrant persons. There are many sex-specific terms in spoken Japanese, not to mention the numerous socially determined ones, to complicate matters for someone as strictly bound to observing social decorum as she was. It must have required a kind of mental gymnastics to try to find the "right words" in translating her thoughts into American English. The much-quoted Virginia Woolf spoke of habits of the mind and the choice of subject matters that hampered the literary output of women writers of her time. Woolf tells us that she had succeeded in killing "The Angel in the House" but that there are still "many ghosts to fight, many prejudices to overcome."

My own struggles in learning Japanese as a small child may be a case in point. I learned quite early that certain forms were correct for my brothers to use but not for me. My three brothers used the first person singular pronoun "*boku*," but when I did so, I was told I mustn't talk "like a boy." Girls must use the more polite form *watashi* in informal conversation, and *watakushi* in formal settings, I was told. In confusion I simply referred to myself by name— "Mitsuye would like a glass of milk." I did not know then it is not necessary to use a pronoun in most verbal constructions in Japanese.

As we grew older, I learned that certain forms of expressions became even more complex, especially for girls. For example, my father simply said "*Hitotsu kure*" (Give [me] one), to my mother at the dinner table. When my brothers and I were quite young, the informal "*Hitostu chodai*" was acceptable, but I soon learned (at about age twelve) that the informal language I had learned as a child is spoken only to one's peers, and since I never spoke Japanese to my brothers or to my friends, a whole new way of speaking, a "ladylike" polite way, to one's superiors had to be learned. And so, instead of *"Hitotsu chodai,"* I was told to say *"Hitostu kudasai masen ka?"* (Won't [you] please give [me] one?) An avid reader of novels in those days, I used to sit at the kitchen table recounting in Japanese the summary plot of the story I happened to be reading while my mother prepared the family dinner.[8] It was a special time for us because my older brothers were outdoors playing and dinner preparation for a full course meal was very often an elaborate ritual for my mother. Suddenly at around age eleven or twelve, the age a girl must become a "lady," I stopped doing this and spoke to her as little as possible in Japanese because of constant unpleasant interruptions. She was not aware that in her effort to teach me the absolutely proper Japanese (so that I would not disgrace myself in public as an adult woman, she said) she not only succeeded in muzzling me, but effectively put a wedge in our relationship which would not be closed for many years.

During my early teens I learned in an interesting way that Japanese men's language is more open and free. As a teenager with literary aspirations, I often sat, enraptured, in our dining room as I watched a group of twenty to thirty poets spending long hours scribbling Japanese characters on strips of paper on their laps. I was not there as a participant at these monthly meetings of my father's poetry society, the Senryu Kai, but as part of the kitchen help, serving tea, makizushi and assorted snacks prepared by my mother. I looked forward to these meetings because of the thrill of watching the calligrapher brush fluid black characters on a long roll of paper pinned on the whole length of our dining room wall. Listening to the poets intone their short lines as the calligrapher made his brush strokes was a special treat for me, though I understood only snatches of the words. After each reading, there would be audible murmurs of appreciation or bursts of laughter.

Senryu's short fourteen syllable verses were written in concrete language with wit and humor about the daily cares and concerns of the poets. The humor was often sardonic, and, I gathered, frequently scatological and bawdy, but as long as I kept a straight face through the "punch lines" as they laughed raucously, my father and his friends assumed that their jokes were slipping by this properly brought-up teenage girl. My mother would call me back into the kitchen from time to time and tell me to do my job and not listen to any of the "male silliness" going on out there in the dining room.

There was one woman in the group, a Mrs. Kawaguchi, but she was so "different" from any Issei woman I knew that I did not consider her sitting there writing senryu among the men at all strange. She out-talked the men in her low raspy voice, laughed out loud with her mouth open, and smoked and drank, just like my father and the other men in the group. My mother and her friends had taught me by example that women should speak with discretion in high-pitched voices and in a childlike manner in the presence of men and must always laugh politely covering their mouths with their hands. And as far as I knew, none of my mother's friends smoked or drank. Furthermore, and more shocking was that Mrs. Kawaguchi talked like the men, using the kind of language Mother would have considered coarse and definitely unladylike. Like my father, she would demand, "*Hitostu kure*" (Give [me] one) as she held out her plate for another helping of sushi to the man at the other end of the table. Not only that, she and the men addressed each other as "*kimi*" (you), a pronoun form I was told I must never use. It is only for boys, I was told, when they talk to each other or for grown men in addressing other males. Or as they gossiped about an absent poet, she would say "anno yatsu" meaning "that person" an especially vulgar expression I was told was only for men. Obviously the men accepted her as one of them, a fellow poet. Mrs. Kawaguchi's presence in our dining room "acting like a man" irritated my mother and fascinated me.

On one occasion when I returned to the kitchen with a pot of tea saying, "Mrs. Kawaguchi says this tea is cold," my mother hissed savagely under her breath, "That woman has two small children at home. What is she doing here in the company of men writing senryu?" To my mother, writing senryu, like drinking and other forms of debauchery, was all right for men, but women, (especially mothers of small children), had more important things to do. I must have looked surprised, more by her tone than her words. Noticing my expression she explained, "She could be writing haiku, at least. Senryu is not for women. Men are 'lousy;' it's their nature." She was speaking Japanese interspersed with English words. I knew she had meant to say "rowdy," and I could not resist breaking into a wide smile as I must have done at her malaprops on many other occasions. I was amused, I remember, by her inadvertent cleverness: senryu is indeed "lousy" because it is boisterous, coarse, repellent, and bad. She immediately directed her anger at me, "And you, a young girl like you shouldn't be standing there '*pok'kan to shite*', like a dummy, listening to such stupidity!" The onomatopoeic Japanese word *pok'kan*, which imitates the hollow sound of an empty vessel might have come right out of one the senryu poems. Its harsh ring used to intimidate me when I was a small child, but I was, by this time, an arrogant high school teenager majoring in English.

By then I was taught the differences between "good" poetry and "bad" poetry in my literature classes, and her words must have reinforced my learning. In my English classes I was reading sonnets by the likes of Shakespeare and John Donne and publishing some of my own in the school creative writing magazine. I must have agreed with her that indulging in expressing one's angers and frustrations using unadorned language or body metaphors was frivolous and vulgar. This particular incident, among all the other Senryu Kai meetings my father had at our house remains vivid in my mind. It must have been the time I had processed the information about "proper" and "improper" language for poetry, especially for women, and came out on the side of "proper" academic poetry. It would take me almost thirty-five years after writing my "camp poems" about my experiences in a concentration camp in Idaho during World War II before I took them to be "serious" poetry. Those poems were not crafted sonnets; neither were they "haiku-like." They were simply notes of everyday happenings I jotted down during my internment, more like my father's senryu.

The language of haiku is symbolic, encoded, implicit; therefore, presumably elegant and ladylike. The language of senryu on the other hand is concrete, direct, explicit; therefore "inelegant." Oddly enough, the mother I knew with only family members present was not ladylike: quiet and demurring. She was commanding, strong, and frequently given to angry outbursts. Ironically, the haiku form which she admired so much would have been too subtle for her to express the intensity of her passions forcefully and directly. Still, she would not have permitted herself to join the men in her own dining room writing senryu alongside Mrs. Kawaguchi. During those Senryu Kai meetings, she demonstrated clearly that she resented the position of serving others who were indulging themselves writing poetry in her dining room, but she kept her anger in check and simmering beneath a swift efficient surface as she worked. I remember trying to keep an emotional as well as a physical distance from her whenever possible during those times, for I knew I would become the target of her anger if I stood around.

Generally speaking, the Nisei, born and raised in a society less bound by class than the Issei and having learned English at a younger age, were not hobbled by old-country traditions. One might assume, then, that the Nisei have been freed of what Tillie Olsen calls the "unnatural silence"[9] imposed by varying sociological and psychological circumstances. Such an assumption would only be partially true judging from the types of writings that the Nisei, as well as children of immigrants from other Asian countries, have traditionally done in the past decades. Personal narratives and imaginative writings would tell us what forced acculturation *feels* like, but the fact is, we have many more historical and sociological studies by Nisei and other scholars about our history than personal accounts or fictional stories that would expose how we feel about our experiences.

Persons who are constantly on the watch about their language form, the way they speak or write, are more likely to guard their thoughts and feelings more carefully. Most Nisei who grew up before World War II will remember that the pressure to learn to speak American English "like a white person" was very great.[10] In fact, some Nisei have deliberately resisted learning Japanese in order to be "more American." Some of us tried to give up our original language because, we were told, hanging onto it would hamper our progress in learning "perfect" English and would make us seem "unAmerican." For us, cutting away the Japanese language from our consciousness seemed a simple way of casting our lot with the American majority. By disassociating ourselves from "alien languages" spoken by our parents and newly arrived Asian immigrants, we believed we were freed of the complex issues of identity that plagued our parents. We were embarrassed by our mothers who, it seemed, were either incapable of learning or refused to learn to speak English. (The fathers, because they were out in the work force, generally spoke communicable English.) Many of us had school friends with European immigrant parents who were adjusting remarkably well; why couldn't our mothers be like them?

Most Nisei could not understand the terror our mothers felt in being forced to reject everything familiar to them. For the most part, our mothers became adjusted to wearing shoes and Western dress, to eating American food, and even to seeing their children rapidly drifting away from them by adopting American ideas and manners. Most of us thought little about the racist nature of the laws aimed specifically at Asian nationals, such as the restrictions against our becoming naturalized U.S. citizens and buying land in this country. We were not sensitive to the notion that our mothers may have been psychologically unwilling to give up what seemed to them the only vestige of their heritage, their native language, that could not be invaded by the foreign culture that surrounded them every day. As products of the American educational system, we Nisei believed in the Protestant work ethic: you can attain anything and get anywhere you want if you work hard enough at it. The corollary to that of course is obvious: it must be your own fault if you aren't getting anywhere.

An incident during World War II would illustrate to what

extent some of us had been indoctrinated and had internalized this old saw. During the planning stage of the removal of the West Coast Japanese to concentration camps a few months following the outbreak of World War II, Milton Eisenhower, then Director of the War Relocation Authority, apparently sought the opinion of one of the older Nisei leaders in the Japanese American community about the management of the Japanese in the camps. In his response to the Director, our "spokesman" suggested that schools should be set up in these camps and include in their curriculum speech classes to eliminate all traces of the "Japanese American accent or mannerisms" so that we would not encounter prejudice against us when we left camp. This notion was alive and well more than three decades later in the 1970's. An enterprising couple in California was advertising in Vietnamese and Korean language newspapers, "Learn to speak American in six weeks! Erase your Asian accent and get higher paying jobs!" "Speak American" became the buzz words. Although quite a number of Vietnamese persons I met during those days spoke functional English, they were led to believe that all their problems would be solved magically and simply if they took this six-week course. Needless to say, this couple did a brisk business.

The enormous success of the "U.S. English" movement, actively supported by the former U.S. Senator S.I. Hayakawa, can be attributed to support from both new and old immigrants as well as the general public. The immigrants have been loathe to express opposition to the English-only movement for fear of appearing anti-American while the non-foreign population has rallied around this issue with a renewed sense of patriotism. It has given the latter an outlet for their resentment against the infusion of Asian immigrants and other refugees in our communities with their various "foreign and alien" languages and cultures.

In 1987 the voters of California in their seeming concern for national unity overwhelmingly passed an "English Only" initiative. This initiative made English the official state language in California and has served to fan the already percolating xenophobia among us. Since the passage of this initiative, there has been a series of troubling incidents such as the disciplinary action against hospital workers at University of California in San Francisco for speaking Spanish and Tagalog to fellow workers and attempts to prevent donations of Chinese language books to the library in a community in Southern California. Such incidents serve to divide us more than bilingualism or multilingualism ever could. The insidiousness of the movement becomes quite apparent. Facility in learning "perfect" English among the newly arrived immigrants has become a measuring stick to test their loyalty to their adopted country.

No one, the recent immigrant least of all, wants to be locked up in what are often referred to as "language ghettos." Most immigrants understand that becoming proficient in English is a way of finding a better way of living in this country. However, the English-only movement is primarily a negative campaign. Its tactics aim to limit the rights of the new immigrants, specifically Latinos and Asians. More damaging than disenfranchising the immigrant population by relegating them to second-class citizenship are attempts to convince them that they are second class people in the eyes of the "world." When children are told in a disapproving way to "speak only in English," they perceive that English is "better." In first grade I was forced to sit crouched in the kneehole of the teacher's desk for hours in punishment for speaking to my brother in Japanese (only a year apart, we started first grade together). Did I know that this was being done "for my own good" so that I would learn English more quickly? Among other things, I learned that speaking Japanese in public leads to humiliation. The lines were clearly drawn. English is like Sunday clothes and is the superior language. By extension I learned that the whites who speak it must be the superior race, and I must learn to speak as the whites do. At that very young age, I was already on my way to what Elizabeth Dodson Gray labels "hierarchical thinking."[11]

Gray, a feminist theologian, believes that we must change the way we think about differences. She writes:

...when we are responding to differences (whether man and woman, or man and whale, or man and chimp, or man and God), our perceptions are dominated and

distorted by the hierarchical paradigm. Almost in the same instant that we perceive difference, we are looking to ascertain rankings of power, moral or economic value, and aesthetic preference. We do this whether it is a different animal, a different culture, or a skin pigmentation that is different.
The hierarchical paradigm... is a veritable contact lens. So intimately is it a part of how we perceive that we seem never to assess difference as just that — different. Instead we insist upon *imposing comparative rankings which are incomplete and often self-serving* (Italics mine).[12]

In her sweeping book on how our religious and cultural attitudes are destroying the environment, Gray writes that diversity in nature is not only desirable but necessary for our survival. With the present interest in cultural diversity, we may be moving in the right direction though, to some of us, it seems at a creeping pace. Many Asian American writers who now speak and write well enough not to be an "embarrassment" to their races have taken on the task of being interpreters of our immigrant parents' experiences and of exploring our own relationships with them. A few of us are published by small presses.[13] Some short prose works have appeared in recent major multi-cultural anthologies.[14] An even smaller minority of Asian writers, most notably Maxine Hong Kingston and Amy Tan, have been published by major publishers.

The recognition that powerful social forces have kept us strangely estranged from our parents' cultural heritages has been a crucial step for us, the second and third generation children of immigrants who are writing today. We must find ways of letting the newer immigrants know that they do not have to wait to completely "master" American English before we will listen to them. We must let them know that there is a down side to being "perfect." Those of us who have been around long enough know about the "model minority" syndrome. We know that the more we strive for "perfection," the more isolated we become.

Nor can we wait for some major American writer to write

for the new immigrants as suggested by Bharati Mukherjee, an East Indian American writer. In an article that appeared in the *New York Times* on the occasion of her becoming "naturalized" (as some wag put it, the foreign-born are "unnatural" until they become naturalized U.S. citizens), this writer of acutely insightful stories about cross-cultural adjustment problems writes, "There is a blind spot in American writing, and even our best writers are guilty of passing over one of the biggest stories in recent American history: While American fiction is sunk in a decade of minimalism, an epic is washing up on its shores." Mukherjee laments the loss of those stories by New Americans who have "lived through centuries of history in a single lifetime" and who are "bursting with stories." She challenges current American authors to awaken to the rich source of materials among the immigrant population.

The loss of those stories is real, but I do not agree with her. I hope that we do not have to wait until some accepted American writer with perfect English adopts the immigrants as interesting subjects before their experiences can be considered "universal" and therefore a bona fide part of American culture. The act of writing itself is a transforming process, as most of us who have taught writing know. Our own writings shape us. There are thousands of immigrant Asians out there who may not know until they are encouraged to write about it what it is that they have to offer us in the Western world. Many of these people come from countries that have been colonized and re-colonized and have seen first-hand what several successive wars in their lifetime have done to their countries. Many of these Asians, unlike the other immigrants before them throughout our history, did not come willingly to better economic conditions. Many of these new immigrants remain here somewhat reluctantly because of political conditions in their own country and, like my mother, are resisting the traditional acculturation process. Their collective experiences could tell us much about the effects of destructive modern politics. They could tell us a great deal about the process of migration. They could tell us something about the psychological effects of inevitable transformation. We should be encouraging them to record their experiences "in their own voice in their own time."

On a global scale, the cult of the "perfect" English language is seen by many in other countries as a form of cultural imperialism. A few years ago when I visited Japan, I met with a group of Japanese feminists in Kyoto, most of whom were teaching at least one course in women's studies in the neighboring colleges. One of the women remarked that the only women among them who get invited to participate in conferences in United States by women's or academic organizations are bilingual Japanese women. As if, she said ruefully, monolingual Japanese are not as politically aware of feminist issues or as well-informed on scholarly topics. Contrary to popular belief, she felt expressing oneself freely in one's native language through a competent translator is preferable to speaking in one's second language. So again, it is perceived even in Japan that we use English proficiency as a measure of intelligence and judge people accordingly.

What will it take for us to create a climate of acceptance and tolerance for differences among us? For one thing we need to release ourselves from this trap of linguistic purism in order to develop a healthy attitude toward the numerous patois around us and accept them as legitimate forms of expression in our culture. We would not be encouraging a "kind of illiteracy," as one of my colleagues said to me recently. (Besides, how many average Americans speak or write "perfect" English?) Instead, our language would be enriched by creative neologisms introduced into it by new immigrants. We should arrive at a level of sophistication where individualistic idioms in whatever form of mixed communicable patois that are among us can be accepted into the language with ease. The human mind is capable of dealing with several levels of expressions, sometimes switching back and forth, at other times all at the same time as those of us who have raised children know.

If we were all to be liberated from this tyranny of hierarchical language, fight those many ghosts, overcome those many prejudices, we will be hearing more from our immigrant Asian sisters as they write about their experiences in their own unique individual voices in all different stages of their development.

NOTES

1 Joan Goulianos, ed., *By Woman Writt: Literature from Six Centuries by and About Women.* Baltimore: Penguin Books, Inc., 1974.

Louise Bernikow, ed., *The World Split Open: Four Centuries of Women Poets in English and America,* 1552-1950. New York: Random House, Inc., 1974.

2 Sandra M. Gilbert and Susan Gubar, eds., New York: W.W. Norton & Company, Inc., 1985.

3 Him Mark Lai, Genny Lim and Judy Young, eds., *Island; Poetry and History of Chinese Immigrants on Angel Island 1910-1940.* San Francisco, Hoc Doi Project, 1980. Distributed by San Francisco Study Center

4 The Japanese terms Issei, Nisei, and Sansei literally mean "first generation," "second generation," and "third generation." Issei generally refers to the immigrants who came to the United States to work, settle and raise their families. The Nisei refer to the American-born and educated children of Issei, and Sansei to their children.

5 Shirley Geok-lin Lim and Mayumi Tsutakawa, *The Forbidden Stitch; An Asian American Women's Anthology.* Corvallis, OR: Calyx Books, 1988.

6 However, writings by Asians, American born and otherwise, have been attracting some attention in academic circles in recent years. A comprehensive bibliography of literature and literary criticism by Asian Americans is now available for scholars: *Asian American Literature: An Annotated Bibliography,* by King-Kok Cheung and Stan Yogi. New York: Modern Language Association, 1989. Available through the Modern Language Association, 10 Astor Place, New York, NY 10003-6981.

7 *Camp Notes and Other Poems.* Berkeley: Shameless Hussy Press, 1976. Distributed by Kitchen Table; Women of Color Press, Latham, NY.

8 Years later after World War II when I returned home from college, my mother told me she saw the film version of *Les Miserables* and

remembered she had heard the story from me during this period. The detail she remembered particularly was the story of the "poor little mother who sold her hair and teeth to keep her baby fed and clothed." She said laughing, "You were too young to understand what you were reading. How indignant you were over the cruelty toward the girl 'just because she had a baby.'"

9 Tillie Olsen, *Silences.* New York: Delacorte Press/ Seymour Lawrence, 1978, p. 6.

10 I must mention that the following discussion reflects the general attitude of the American-born Nisei, although I am technically not a Nisei, having been born in Japan. As a child of Issei parents and someone who was primarily educated in the United States, I speak from the Nisei point of view. On the other hand, because I grew up as a Japanese national, like my parents, I was more aware of the Issei's sensitivities than the average Nisei. We were barred by law from becoming a naturalized United States citizen until the passage of the Walter McCarran Immigration and Naturalization Act of 1953 when I was thirty years old.

11 Elizabeth Dodson Gray, *Green Paradise Lost.* Wellesley, MA: Roundtable Press, 1981, p. 20.

12 Gray, p. 11.

13 Among them *Seventeen Syllables and Other Stories* by Hisaye Yamamoto just published by Kitchen Table; Women of Color Press.

14 For example, Merle Woo's "Letter to Ma" in *New Worlds of Literature*, an anthology of multi-cultural writers recently published by W.W. Norton.

Songs Of Owl Woman

by Helen Jaskoski

Introduction

The O'odham live in southern Arizona and northern Mexico, in desert country that appears barren and forbidding to the stranger. They used to be known by the name Papago, but have now decided to use their own word for themselves, O'odham, "The People." The people have lived here for hundreds of years, and all their arts reflect their intimate relationship with this landscape and environment, like no other on earth.

According to O'odham poet and linguist Ofelia Zepeda, the people did not have what Europeans call poetry among their traditional art forms. Rather, they had, and have, many songs. Songs are a special form of verbal discourse: there is a special language just for songs, including vocabulary different from the language used in ordinary speech. O'odham artists traditionally received their songs in dreams. Danny Lopez, another O'odham poet, encourages song-dreamers now to compose as their ancestors did. Both Ofelia Zepeda and Danny Lopez also encourage the people to compose poetry in everyday language, written and spoken words.

Owl Woman and Francis Densmore

In the 1920s a musicologist named Frances Densmore traveled to Arizona to record songs. Densmore had previously made transcriptions and, with the help of tribal people, translations of song texts from peoples of the Chippewa, Sioux and Nootka, among others. The result of her work was published in 1929 in "Papago Music," Bulletin 90 of the Smithsonian Institution's Bureau of American Ethnology.

147

In the course of her work, Densmore met and worked with a remarkable woman doctor who treated the sick according to traditional methods: with singing and ceremony. This was Owl Woman, whom outsiders knew as Juana Manuel. Owl Woman was already an old woman when Densmore met her; she was living near Mission San Francisco Xavier, which is on a small Papago reservation just outside Tucson. Owl Woman had an assistant, Sivariano Garcia, to whom she had taught many of her songs, who helped her in her curing, and who recorded her songs for Frances Densmore.

This is Densmore's description of Owl Woman and her singing: "The spirits first revealed themselves to Owl Woman when she was in extreme grief over the death of her husband and other relatives. This was 30 or 40 years prior to the recording of her songs in 1920. The spirits took her to the spirit land in the evening and brought her back in the early dawn, escorting her along a road. They took her to a high place from which she could see the abode of the spirits, and her dead relatives came one at a time to talk with her. If too many had come at once they would have taken her back with them. In these meetings she found her relatives happy and looking neither younger nor older than in life. The spirit land, into which she looked, was thickly populated, the people living 'on the ground,' as in the old times, and not in houses. She saw blackish waters, beside which the children played. The spirits danced during the night, enjoying the same pleasures as when they were on earth.

"When the spirits had taken her many times to their abode and had shown her many things they decided that she should be taught certain songs for the cure of sickness caused by the spirits. It was not necessary that she should go to the spirit land to learn the songs. It was decided that a person, at his death, should go where the other spirits are and 'get acquainted a little,' after which he would return and teach her some songs...

"The phonographic recording of Owl Woman's songs occupied an entire day. She did not wish to sing into the phonograph and insisted that Garcia record the songs. She sang each song softly in order to recall it to his mind, and toward the latter part of the day she sang with him, but not loud enough for her voice to be recorded. At the beginning of the day, when telling of her visits to the spirit world, she had the appearance of a sibyl, with a strange, far-seeing look in her eyes. The day was chilly and in addition to the white head covering worn by the Papago women, she wore her black shawl wrapped tightly around her... In the first two hours Garcia's interest did not falter and he sang one song after another at her dictation. But there came a time when he left out two or three words. There was much talking in Papago. The old woman was suddenly full of animation and fire. The interpreter said, 'She is telling him that he must not be discouraged because he forgot those words. She says he must go on as if nothing had happened.' Garcia rallied to his task and the work continued, but the old woman gave closer attention to her singer. Even to one who did not understand the language it was evident that she was encouraging him and holding his interest. She was bright, active, with an occasional witticism at which they laughed heartily. At the close of the afternoon Garcia was singing steadily with little sign of weariness but her face was drawn and tired, as of one who had been under a long strain. How many long nights she had held her singers at their task by the force of personality, while she watched the flickering life of a sick man!"

Owl Woman's Songs for Healing the Sick

I. "In the Blue Night"

How shall I begin my song
In the blue night that is settling?
I will sit here and begin my song.

Densmore says that this song was given to Owl Woman by a man who had been killed near Tucson: "He came to Owl Woman's house one night and told her not to be sad any more about her dead relatives, and said that if any of the people were sick she would have songs with which to cure them."
After that night, he gave Owl Woman two songs. Owl

Woman told Frances Densmore that this was one of the songs with which she customarily began her night-long treatment. "Each of the four parts of the night has its own songs, which are in groups of four and are sung in sequence."

This poem sounds like a traditional invocation to the muses, as the classical Greek poets used to begin an epic. Owl Woman's night-long treatment of her patient was a journey, in which she followed their souls and brought them back to he land of the living. An epic beginning is appropriate. The curing ceremony is really one long poem.

"The blue night": a being, settling on the land. I was born where Owl Woman lived. The sky is immense here, though the valley is ringed by mountains. The mountains go pink, scarlet, fuchsia at sunset, and turn a darker blue than the sky, which darkens to match their cobalt, finally black color.

II. "In the Dark I Enter"

I can not make out what I see.
In the dark I enter.
I can not make out what I see.

This song was the gift of an old man, Nonka Simapere, who had died suddenly. Densmore says of the melody that "there is a groping and lack of decision in the melody which is interesting in connection with its title." There are no original-language texts in Densmore's document, so we do not know if the chorus was repeated exactly, as here, or not.

Urban dwellers forget how dark the night is when no artificial illumination exists. Helen Sekaquaptewa, a Hopi woman who had been kidnaped as a child and taken to boarding school, thought it was daylight when she woke up to electric lights for the first time.

The poem tells us that death is the entrance to new life. When I read "I can not make out what I see" it reminds me of students, trying to comprehend a text. Or being in a foreign country: when I first entered Poland and Greece, I could understand none of the street signs. So often I have felt that I cannot make out what I see. We enter in darkness, groping.

Philosophers and psychoanalysts will say that the poem expresses the Socratic journey to self-knowledge. For them, all knowledge is self-knowledge. Owl Woman might not have seen it so differently: she had to know herself and her patients, and the spirits who brought her songs.

III. "Yonder Lies the Spirit Land"

Yonder lies the spirit land.
Yonder the spirit land I see.
Farther ahead, in front of me,
I see a spirit stand.

Densmore says that eight years before recording this song, Owl Woman went to see a young man named Jose Louis, who was sick. It was very late when she started home again, and on her way she met a young man. She noticed that this was one of Jose's friends who had died. Jose was taken to a ranch and died soon afterwards. A few days later, he returned and gave Owl Woman this song and another one.

Harry Encinas of San Xavier translated Owl Woman's songs. He had been a student at Carlisle, and here he conveys some of the original's artistry in his use of chiasmic rhyme. The repetition of "yonder" and "farther ahead" suggests the distance the soul is traveling on this journey to the land of the dead; the motion itself is communicated in the progression as the song moves us from knowing where the spirit land is, to seeing it, to seeing, finally, one of its inhabitants.

IV. "We Will Join Them"

Yonder are spirits laughing and talking as though drunk.
They do the same things that we do.
Now we will join them.

Densmore: "One day as Owl Woman was resting by a hill a spirit came to her. It was that of a man who died eight years previously, and his sister who died at about the same time was with him. The two were riding on one horse. The man said he had just come back to see the condition of his house. He asked what she was doing and she replied that she was going after wood and had sat down to rest. He taught her this song."

We create our gods, our heaven and our hells, out of the image we have of ourselves. How familiar, how comfortable, death may be, to the person familiar and comfortable with life. Dante saw the company of the dead whom he hoped to join as a mystical rose. Here, death is a party among family and friends. Of course one would like to join in.

V. Untitled

In the great night my heart will go out,
Toward me the darkness comes rattling,
In the great night my heart will go out.

These words were, Densmore said, translated freely, but without the melody which she found "lacking in interest." Now, the federal government is making the old wax cylinder and wire recordings available to tribal peoples, so they can learn and use the songs again. Owl Woman said that Jose Gomez, the young boy who gave her the song after he died, was "slow and sleepy headed."

Densmore is not the only one to freely translate this text. Another anthologizer changed "rattling" to "rustling," and his version found its way into many other reprints. "Rattling" makes more sense to someone born where Owl Woman lived: rattlesnakes live there, and they do look around at night. I know a nurse who worked many years at Saint Mary's Hospital in Tucson. She told a story once about treating a man from the reservation for snakebite. He had been on his way back from the outhouse at night when the snake bit him on the leg. He was a veteran, an amputee; he said, "If only I had put the wooden leg out first."

The night is great. The song acknowledges the local physical darkness, and that larger darkness beyond the small darkness of night and sleep. John Donne said: "I run to death, and death meets me as fast." He felt his heart going out.

VI. "I Am Going to See the Land"

I am going far to see the land,
I am running far to see the land,
While back in my house the songs are intermingling.

Densmore tells us that this song is part of the group sung just before midnight. This is the most delicate part of the long curing process, when the doctor is most vulnerable. The text is the song of a journey to the land of the spirits. All of the people involved in the ceremony are singing. Densmore says the group of fifteen or twenty singers "usually spend an entire night with a sick person and by morning he is perceptibly better or else she knows that she can not help him. She uses certain songs for the beginning of the treatment, others are sung shortly before midnight, others after midnight, and still others as the day is breaking." Each singer has a gourd rattle.

The person who is sick is making the journey to recover his or her soul. The patient runs, yet remains at home, hearing the songs. I think of these songs within; no matter how far away from home, one hears that harmony.

The songs of Owl Woman are a tiny part of the rich literature of the O'odham Papago people. Owl Woman and her assistant, Sivariano Garcia, who sang the songs for Frances Densmore, generously shared their gift. I am grateful to them.

SUGGESTED READINGS

Bahr, Donald. *Pima and Papago Ritual Oratory.* San Francisco: Indian Historian Press, 1975.

Densmore, Frances. *Papago Music.* Bulletin 90, Bureau of American Ethnology. Washington, D.C. Government Printing Office, 1929.

Evers, Larry, editor. *The South Corner of Time.* Tucson: University of Arizona Press, 1981.

Underhill, Ruth. *Papago Woman.* New York: Holt Rinehart & Winston, 1979.

Underhill, Ruth. *Singing for Power: The Song Magic of the Papago Indians.* Berkeley: University of California Press, 1938.

*"A community... is an
ordering of sister-relationships."*

Paula Gunn Allen

Biographical Notes

Kelli Arakaki-Bond is a computer/corporate communications consultant who holds a degree in communications from California State University, Fullerton. She also teaches English and word processing at the Southern California College of Business and Law. An associate editor of *The Webs We Weave,* Orange County's first comprehensive poetry anthology, she has been published in *Common Lives, CQ: The California State Poetry Quarterly, Electrum* and others. Her "24 Karat Poetry: The Bard Behind the Orange Curtain" program originally aired in July 1989 on KPFK Pacifica Radio.

Diana Azar was born in Shanghai, grew up in the San Fernando Valley, and holds degrees in English from UCLA and Columbia University. Her poetry and fiction have appeared in *Mustard Seed, The Elephant-ear, South Coast Poetry Journal,* the *Dan River Anthologies,* and the *Albany Review. Looking for the Worm,* a collection of short stories was published by Dan River Press in 1989. Diana leads a creative writing workshop in Laguna Beach, and is on the writing staff at Irvine Valley College in Irvine, California,.

Alane Hayes, resident of Orange County for 13 years, hails from Cleveland, Ohio. Her love of literature began after reading the works of Maya Angelou and James Baldwin, and more recently, Audre Lorde and Barbara Smith. Alane is pursuing a bachelor's degree in English at California State University, Fullerton. She would like to increase the awareness of contributions of African-American writers. Alane is currently employed as a medical transcriptionist.

Sarie Sachie Hylkema was born Sarie Sachie Munemitsu in Lahaina, Maui, Hawaii where she lived until she entered college in the state of Michigan. With her family which included two children, Eric and Denise, she moved to Costa Mesa in November, 1962 where she still resides. Sarie is currently the Special Assistant to the Associate Dean of Academic Administration of the University of California Irvine, College of Medicine. She is one of the founding members of MCWW and is published in *The Webs We Weave; Orange County Poetry Anthology.* She is committed to supporting and empowering women, especially Asian American women, in their discovery of their selves.

Helen Jaskoski: "Place and landscape are important to me. I was born and grew up in Arizona, a beautiful and demanding landscape. But the cities that appear most often in my dreams are European cities I have lived in: Lublin, Poland and Florence, Italy. I've done a lot of different kinds of work: farm worker, musician, nurse's aid, and technical writer. Education has been precious: sometimes it has meant choosing between buying food or books. Now I think I'm very fortunate to be able to teach: literature is one thing I love, and I like to share my pleasure in it." Helen Jaskoski has lectured on Ethnic Literature in Florence, Milan, Romania and Poland. She has a Ph.D. from Stanford University and teaches literature at California State University, Fullerton.

Janet Jue, a second generation Chinese American, was born in Bakersfield, California. (Bakersfield was once a railroad stop where her grandfather cooked for the railroad workers in the late 1800's.) Janet is one of the founding members of MCWW. Currently, she is the coordinator of the Visual Arts Department at Fountain Valley High School where she has been teaching art and English since 1973. She lives in Laguna Beach with her husband, Ken, and their two school-aged children, Jennifer and Christopher.

Florinda Mintz read for the first time in public when she was 17 years old on Radio Municipal, Buenos Aires, Argentina. Her first book of poetry, *Oracion Profana* was published in 1978. She has been published in various publications in Argentina, Uruguay, Spain and U.S.A. She is a judge for the Chicano Literary Contest of the Spanish and Portuguese Department of the University of California, Irvine. She writes a column on performing arts, literature, community events and interviews for *Azteca News,* generating news information. She works directly in researching and editing material to be published. In 1988, she became a free lance reporter for *La Nacion,* the major newspaper in Buenos Aires, Argentina.

Priscilla Oaks was a Professor of English in the English Department at California State University, Fullerton. She was awarded a Fulbright Fellowship in 1980 and spent two years teaching in the People's Republic of China. She was the author of *Ethnic Studies: An Annotated Bibliography* and co-editor of *Harvest,* a book of interviews of Orange County minorities. Her last critical essay, "Orange County Immigrant Literature: Asian Pacific Writers" was published in *Second Lives* by the South Coast Repertory in 1983. She was an active member of MELUS, Society for the Study of of the Multi-Ethnic Literature of the United States.

Susana Saladini was born in Argentina a long time ago. She came to the United States at the age of 25, a teacher with a bachelor's degree in theater. She worked in many different jobs to support herself and her young daughter. As motel maid, housekeeper, office assistant, Spanish instructor, etc. Susana learned a great deal about human behavior, and especially about the struggle of being a young female in a world "temporarily" controlled by males. Susana studied English at Orange Coast College as well as on her own. She is "autodidacta." She writes from her own observations and her experiences. A cheerful and dynamic feminist with a great sense of humor, she is convinced that a better world can only be achieved by worldwide overall female government helped by males. She is presently working as elementary school teacher.

Mitsuye Yamada, founder of Multi-Cultural Women Writers is Emerita Professor of English from Cypress College where she taught for twenty-three years. Currently she is doing the Southern California university circuit as Visiting Professor in creative writing and Asian American literature. She has a B.A. from New York University and an M.A. from the University of Chicago. Her publications include *Camp Notes and Other Poems* (Shameless Hussy Press/1976); *The Webs We Weave* (Co-editor, Literary Arts Press/1986); and *Desert Run; Poems and Stories* (Kitchen Table: Women of Color Press/1988.) She was a recipient of the Vesta Award (Woman's Building, Los Angeles/1982) and was awarded a writer's residency from Yaddo (Saratoga Springs, NY/1984). She and Nellie Wong are the subjects of a film, *Mitsuye and Nellie: Asian American Poets* (Light/Saraf Films/1984). She serves on the Board of Directors of Amnesty International.

Kanwal Yodh was born in British India, educated in India, Pakistan and the United States. She taught biology and general science in the subcontinent before returning to the United States in 1958 as an immigrant. She has sought to bring awareness of problems women and immigrants face. In the narrative essay in this collection she describes her experiences in finding placement in the American system in her chosen field. She contributed a column to a Toronto-based local newspaper of the Indo-Pak community. This column dealt with problem solving in adjusting to new situations for immigrant women. Now retired, she resides with her physicist husband in Irvine, California, and spends time volunteering for the seniors, writing and painting.

SOWING TI LEAVES

WRITINGS BY MULTICULTURAL WOMEN

☐ Yes, please send me more *Sowing Ti Leaves (160pp.)*

_____ Book(s)	@ $7.95 each	_____
CA tax	(62¢ per each book.)	_____
Postage	($1.50 for first book, Add 50¢ for each add'l book.)	_____
	Total Enclosed	$ _____

Name _____

Organization _____

Street _____

City _____ State _____ Zip _____

Phone _____

Please make check payable to MCWW. Send to:

MCWW
6151 Sierra Bravo Rd
Irvine CA 92715